Keeping a Princess Heart
in a
Not-So-Fairy-Tale World

NICOLE JOHNSON

THOMAS NELSON
Since 1798

NASHVILLE   DALLAS   MEXICO CITY   RIO DE JANEIRO   BEIJING

Published in Nasville, Tennessee. Thomas Nelson is a trademark of Thomas Nelson, Inc.

Thomas Nelson, Inc. titles may be purchased in bulk for educational, business, fund-raising, or sales promotional use. For information, please e-mail SpecialMarkets@ThomasNelson.com.

Library of Congress Cataloging-in-Publication Data
Johnson, Nicole, 1966–
Keeping a princess heart in a not so fairy tale world / by Nicole Johnson.
p. cm.
ISBN 10: 0-8499-1881-2 (trade paper)
ISBN 13: 978-0-8499-1881-0 (trade paper)
ISBN: 0-8499-1788-3 (hardcover)
1. Christian women—Religious life. I. Title.
BV4527.J638 2003
248.8'43–dc21
2003004901

Printed in the United States of America
08 09 10 11 RRD 9 8 7 6 5 4 3

for the Prince, with love

CONTENTS

CONTENTS

The Princess in Pajamas

Callie Randall fell fast asleep with her tiara slightly crooked and just a little bit tangled in her blond hair. It had been a very busy day for the princess. Riding her bike to strange new lands, negotiating a peace treaty with the neighbors' dog, reclaiming palace treasures that lay hidden and nearly forgotten in the tall grass, and even being an ambassador of goodwill to her brother (not a prince), Nathan.

After all, there was a lot of catching up to do.

It had been barely a week since her father had placed the little tiara on her head.

"It's beautiful," she had whispered in awe as he pulled it from his black suitcase that lay open on the bed. "Is it real?" She was kind of out of breath and scared to ask.

"Of course," her daddy whispered back close to her cheek as he gave her a quick kiss. "It belonged to a princess in Seattle, where I had to go for business this week." He turned the glorious little crown this way and that, angling it just *right to catch the light, making it sparkle. Callie was in a happy trance under its dazzling spell.*

Her mother smiled in the doorway.

Her father dropped to one knee, cleared his throat, and said in his most serious voice, "Callie." He took his time with each word. "You are a princess."

Then he did the funniest thing. He went to his briefcase and pulled a piece of paper from the many that were sticking out all over, and he rolled it up and put it to his mouth. "Doot-doot-doo!" he trumpeted. "Announcing Princess Callie!" And he placed the tiny, glittering tiara very carefully on her head.

Callie stood straight up on her tiptoes to receive the crown. Every muscle in her little body was stretched taut as she walked slowly around the room, afraid her crown might fall off. Her six-year-old posture was perfect, and her tiny neck felt a full two inches longer carrying its precious cargo. Her arms were stiff as rods by her side, and for no real reason, her pinkie fingers stuck straight out. "I'm a princess," she said out loud and managed a twirl and a half on the hardwood floor. "I'm a princess," she giggled, "a princess in my pajamas!"

For six days the princess and her tiara had seldom parted. And behind the soft green eyes now closed in slumber, Callie Randall dreamed of castles, princes, and horse-drawn carriages. Meanwhile, in the bedroom next door, burgundy loafer heels clicked on the hardwood floor as Callie Randall's daddy packed his black suitcase for the last time.

She awoke with a start. Her heart was racing. Her hair was stuck with sweat around her neck. The cotton tee she'd worn to bed was twisted halfway around her body, and her stomach was bare and cold. She stared hard into the blackness of the hotel room, trying to remember where she was. Room 6-something, but what city? Oh yeah, Atlanta. *Franklin Howard Company. That was why she was here, consulting.*

Awful day. Two glasses of Cabernet before bed hadn't made it any better, and now she had a thick, dry tongue and a slight headache. Her bladder was full, but she didn't move. The air conditioner cycled on, and a door somewhere down the hall clicked loudly. She wondered what time it was but didn't turn her head toward the clock. Her eyes were boring a hole in the darkness. I must have had a bad dream. *Her heartbeat was slowing back down, and the sweat was making her cold on the back of her neck. She blinked. Her eyelids were dry. She needed to go to the bathroom, and she wanted to check the time. She did neither.*

The words of an old song that Paul Simon sang washed over her. A good day ain't got no rain. . . . A bad day is when I lie in bed and think of things that might have been. *The tender prick of a tear stung her eye. She felt paralyzed except for the movement of a tiny droplet sliding toward her matted hair.* Slip sliding away. *It didn't matter what time it was; it was gonna be a long night. The bad*

3

events of her life liked to sneak up on her, throw a dark cloth over her head, and hold her hostage until she was gutted by guilt.

Her divorce from Daniel had been a punishing, humiliating failure. A scarlet letter of a different sort—a big red F instead of the familiar A. At least an affair would have meant she'd gotten an A in something. Then there was the issue of the gaping hole left by the loss of her father. If the only man who has ever loved you walks out of your life, isn't it just possible that you weren't enough to keep him there? Usually this litany of regrets was followed by a full-blown self-mugging for the workaholic she'd become.

You're always trying to prove something to someone—you never know when to stop. What are you, a machine? *Voices of accusation. Of self-pity. Of regret. She wondered which voice was coming first for her tonight.* Slip sliding away. *She straightened out her stiff legs (too much running), untwisted her tee-shirt, and hoped desperately that the tears wouldn't overtake her before she could put together some lame rebuttal.* Have mercy, *she prayed to no one in particular. She curled her body into a tiny scared ball and waited.*

It was strangely silent in room 6-something. The familiar attackers didn't come. No distant hoofbeats, no warships on the horizon. Stillness. And an odd sense of peace. Callie lay there in the dark. Where were the voices? Not that she missed them, but this was most unusual. Who was she to argue?

She dragged herself out of bed, headed to the bathroom,

sat down on the toilet, and hung her head. The hotel tile was cold on her bare feet. She blew her nose and stared at the mirror in the dark, seeing way more than she saw in the light—a face too old for thirty-four years. She went back to the bedroom and fished in her black suitcase for socks and pajama bottoms.

Where had the princess gone? Surely her father had lied to her twenty-eight years before. It was that simple. She'd never really been a princess. Daniel hadn't even known what a princess was. And her job gave no allowances for princesses—work, work, and work. She'd become a nine-to-lifer. She'd either been robbed of her princessness, or she'd never really been one. It had worn off. The spell had been broken; the magic didn't work. She sat at the desk there in the dark, wondering, Which is worse, illusion or the death of illusion?

Then a jeering voice echoed in her head. What do you care about being a princess? If you were a princess, you'd just think you had more reasons to be cold and demanding and self-centered. You want your way, Callie, and you don't care what it does to others. Who really wants to be a princess anyway?

"I do." *Another voice she hardly recognized creaked out of her throat.* "God, please, I do."

Yes, she was talking to herself. Well-acquainted with her own internal monologue, she could have full-scale conversations by herself. But then a new voice interrupted.

"Callie." He took his time with each word. "You are a princess."

5

It had to be the voice of her daddy. Searing hot pain on her insides gave way to raw longing. Why did you leave me? You called me a princess; you lied to me. I'm no princess! *She started crying.* Oh, God. Oh, God, help me. *She slumped to the floor.* I am not a princess. Not anymore. I'm thirty-four years old. Why did you leave me?

"Callie." He took his time with each word. "You are a princess."

Who was it? If it wasn't her father, then who? A strange awareness illuminated her thoughts. Surely not. God? Could it be the voice of God? In a flash, she knew it was. But she didn't believe in God. . . . until this very moment. There were many things Callie Randall hadn't believed in until she could no longer disbelieve. She should have been born in the Show Me State of Missouri. Still, this time, something inside her just knew.

The warm touch of love that had eluded her for so long melted over her heart—the kind of love she had never found within herself. God knows she'd tried hard enough. Or found in the arms of a man—Daniel could vouch for the failure of that one. This world takes; it doesn't give. How can love really be of this world? Love must come from something beyond us. *A yearning she had never been able to express suddenly found a voice of its own.* There must be a God, *she thought.*

Then she actually laughed out loud. Who else could call you a princess and really mean it?

All those late-night arguments in bars over the existence of God seemed absolutely silly in the light of the love that was washing over her. New tears began to fall down her cheeks. If there was love, there was also forgiveness for all she'd done wrong. Blessed, quiet acceptance. It felt so good to Callie to cry and then to laugh—so simple and so good. There is a God, *she thought, and although she felt as strange as ever thinking it, she thought that whoever God was, he'd just named her a princess.*

SHE HAD NO IDEA *when she had stopped crying and laughing and had fallen back asleep on the floor. But when Callie awoke again, the clock said 8:22* A.M. *And when she opened the door of room 6-something, she looked directly into the eyes of a man standing across the hall picking up his morning paper. She couldn't have surprised him more as the words tumbled out of her mouth, "I'm a princess."*

He smiled slowly and nodded politely while backing through his doorway. It took him a minute to settle on a response. "Congratulations," he said. Still nodding, he quickly closed the door.

Callie never heard him. She wasn't talking to him anyway. "I'm a princess," she whispered to herself back inside her room. This changed everything. She stood straight up, pointed her toes, stiffened her back, and stuck her pinkies straight out. Perfect thirty-four-year-old posture. For the first time since her daddy had called her a princess, Callie Randall felt like one. She radiated love from the nucleus of her womanly soul. It felt so good. So full, so rich.

"Thank you," she said softly from a very deep place. For

the first time in years, she beamed. "I'm a princess . . . a princess in my pajamas." Such as they were.

Callie Randall fell asleep that night with the tiara slightly crooked and a lot tangled in her blond hair. It had been a busy day for the princess. Flying home across country, returning to a familiar land, negotiating a peace treaty with the rental car agent who had no cars available, returning to the palace to hunt for a very specific treasure buried deep in the attic and found glittering softly at the bottom of the last box she came to. Even being an ambassador of goodwill as she telephoned her brother (still not a prince) after ten years of silence.

After all, there was a lot of catching up to do.

CHAPTER ONE

Once upon a Time

Once upon a time . . . we were little girls. By day we read from our books of fairy tales, and by night we dreamed of the way our lives would turn out. On Sunday nights we parked in our pajamas two inches away from the television. Tinkerbell would fly out waving her wand and putting fairy dust on all the letters on the screen, signifying that the magic was about to begin. The music would swell, and we would hold our breath with excitement as we watched our favorite stories unfold . . .

Cinderella arrived at the ball, and everyone recognized her as a true princess, and we just knew our day to go to the ball was coming . . .

Sleeping Beauty was sleeping beautifully, dreaming of her prince, and we dreamed of the day that our prince would come . . .

Snow White was singing as she got the dwarfs off to

work, and we imagined humming a happy tune, getting our children off to school . . .

We dreamed of beautiful castles, knowing in our hearts that we would one day ride off in a white carriage and live happily ever after . . .

Do you ever wonder, *What happened?* Does it seem that somewhere among the prince, the kids, the laundry, and the carpool the fairy-tale company must have been bought out and is now bankrupt? Does it seem that life played a cruel trick on us? Most of us would openly acknowledge that what we ended up with is so very different than our dreams. It's not exactly like we really were Snow White or Cinderella or Sleeping Beauty. But please, shouldn't there be a few recognizable parallels?

This is where the voice of reason reminds us we can't compare our lives to theirs because they were fairy-tale women in very different times. Theirs would be totally different stories if they had to face what we do today. Walt's women wouldn't have it so easy if they had to make it in today's world.

Can't you just see Cinderella on the Stairmaster trying to keep those thighs firm? She's out of breath, talking on her cell phone: "I'll be there as soon as I can, Charming. I have to finish my workout and then stop by the grocery and pick up the flowers for the table. Will the carriage be arriving at six?"

What about Sleeping Beauty, propped up in bed on all

her pillows, talking anxiously on the phone? "No, Mother, you didn't wake me. I can't sleep. No, I haven't heard from the prince yet, so don't ask me about it. Yes, I'm sure he's still coming."

Or Snow White, sitting in a tangle of computer wires, writing the Christmas letter? "Sleepy is in the second grade now and stays awake through fourth period. We're so proud of him. Grumpy is taking his Ritalin, and it's really helping him."

It would be interesting to watch each of *them* face some of *our* struggles and try to stay positive in our over-whelmingly negative world. Let them deal with the reality of the modern world. Too often we can't tell whether what we are doing matters, and our hopeful hearts grow weary and defeated. Nowadays when we watch those fairy tales with our kids or grandkids, we feel more like the wicked stepmother than the woman with the dreams. If we were to ask, "Mirror, Mirror on the wall, who's the fairest of them all?" it would probably answer, "Stop asking me! It's not you, for crying out loud."

I wonder if our legendary three would begin to feel the drain that so many of us feel—as if life has passed us by, and we'll never have our dream life. Would they, too, feel despair lurking around each corner and face the strong temptation to give up? Too tired to keep their hearts from getting cynical, they might start thinking, *What is the use? Why bother? It's all gone wrong anyway. I quit!*

Then we might see that . . .

11

Cinderella is lying on the couch in her therapist's office. She is complaining and crying loudly, "I know he was a prince when I married him, but he certainly isn't one anymore."

Sleeping Beauty is still in her bedroom, propped up on her pillows and talking on the phone, but this time to the pharmacist. "Yes, this is Sleeping Beauty again. If you could just give me something . . . No, I don't have a prescription. I'm supposed to be asleep!"

Snow White is running full speed through the living room with a frying pan, yelling at the dwarfs, "Close that door! How many times do I have to tell you, we are not air-conditioning the mines?"

Walt Disney didn't do us any favors, or at least it feels that way on most days. Snow White, Cinderella, and Sleeping Beauty seem to point the way to a life we could never really have, yet it's obviously one we continue hoping for anyway. As adult women we are wide awake, facing the loss of our dreams, with no idea what will take their place.

Walt's imagination fed the hunger of our young hearts by promising what we wanted more than anything: *happily ever after.* His sweet stories suggested we would be recognized and loved by those around us, would marry a wonderful prince, and would live in a fabulous castle with flowers constantly blooming in the window boxes. It was just what we wanted and just what we hoped to have. But Walt never gave us a clue about what to do when it went wrong. Susie Bogguss, a country singer, put her question directly to the fabled princess,

> Hey, Cinderella, what's the story all about?
> I've got a funny feeling we missed a page or two
>   somehow.
> Oh, Cinderella, maybe you could help us out.
> Does the shoe fit you now?

So does the shoe still fit? Some days we feel so far away from our original dreams that we fear we've been tricked and taken to some other life (without our written consent). We think sarcastically, *This is not what I signed up for.* No, Walt never wrote anything about how to hold on to beauty or hope or grace when disappointment silently slips handcuffs around your dreams and leads them down the steps to a very dark dungeon.

People wrongly assume that these kinds of questions or feelings of discontent only start to surface around midlife. That's often the case, but a crisis is created when loss starts stealing our dreams, no matter what our age is. Twenty-something songwriter John Mayer coined the term "quarter-life crisis" because he found disappointment to be no respecter of age.

The hard truth is, many of us have watched our dreams die before our very eyes—the desperately longed-for child we could never have, the marriage that didn't survive despite the agony of trying, the illness that stole away a parent or a friend. In the wake of such losses, we seem to have no choice but to trudge on, day after day, through a life quite different than the one we imagined we would have.

WHAT WE LONG FOR VS. WHAT WE LIVE WITH

Man is the only animal that laughs and weeps,
for he is the only animal that is struck with the difference
between what things are and what they should be.
—WILLIAM HAZLITT

Hazlitt is right. The world is not what it should be. Singer Natalie Imbruglia put it this way: "Illusion never changed into something real. I'm wide awake and I can see the perfect sky is torn." She's right too. We are living underneath a very torn sky.

On one side are all the dreams of our hearts and, on the other, all the difficult realities of our lives. We are split between what we wanted and what we got. What we hoped for and what we have. What we longed for and what we live with. Surely there is something more than treading water in the gulf of disappointment between the two.

The evidence of the torn sky is all around us. Turn on the radio, and you hear a lyric full of love and hope in relationship, and the very next song is full of the hate and rage of having to survive alone. Compare two women's magazines—one will have flowers and beautiful scenery promising the fulfillment of all your dreams, and the other will ditch the flowers, trying to appeal to you, the "smart" woman, by telling you to wake up and take what you want from this world. Go to two different movies in a week. One will be a warm romantic comedy of boy meets girl and the other a cold, crushing drama of a misspent life.

The good news is we're not crazy. And we are not alone in our struggle. Every woman is internally wrestling with the same challenge of how to keep her dreams alive. It's the match of the century—the Perfect World vs. the Real World. Which will win our hearts? It's a universal tug of war of spiritual proportions. Every day the back-and-forth continues, generating enough force to make us wonder if we will survive.

LIVING IN A "PERFECT" WORLD

In a valiant effort to keep our dreams alive, it's easy to hold on to the *illusion* of our dreams instead. And the difference between the two is enormous. We rightly want to defy the disappointments and pain of the world by trying to create a better world, more like the fairy tales of our youth. But instead of cultivating the good things from the heart of a true fairy tale, we may create a saccharin kingdom of illusion and denial—a pseudo-Eden where we refuse to allow clouds to rain on our parade.

Along come a score of glossy magazines and the

world's ideal of a "happy homemaker" to help us. This not-so-good fairy godmother shows us how to go from rags to riches and from oven to table. Arriving in her own pumpkin carriage, she steps out of it and turns it into a glorious centerpiece. Forget the prince; the glass slipper now holds floating camellias. She'll even have the wicked stepmother hand dipping candles for the entryway. There is no escaping her constant directions for perfection. On television, in our magazines, plastered on billboards, she gives complete, step-by-step, do-it-yourself guides, straight to the most perfect world you can imagine. Yes, you too can make everything from scratch, including guilt. And no magic wand is necessary.

We soak it up like sponges. We desire to be surrounded by beauty and goodness, but we settle for control and pretense. We demonstrate that we have gulped down the "image is everything" message by spending our money on self-indulgences that affect how we are seen by others, while neglecting the inside issue of who we really are.

Advertisers have figured this out. They play on our not-so-secret desire for this glorious, perfect world, and their promises of perfection bombard us by the hour. Airbrushed faces sell us on perfect skin. Fitness models promote perfect bodies. "Don't give up!" these perfect images seductively whisper to us. "You can be better. You, too, can have the perfect body, the perfect lawn, the perfect husband, or even the perfect affair" (depending on which magazines you read or shows you watch). We are obsessed with the perfect anything. We don't care what it is as long as it is the best. We live in the modern world, and we can buy anything and everything from the perfect place right up to the perfect face.

But building castles in the air is a little like holding a fake smile. It looks pleasant until your mouth starts to hurt, and your dishonesty is exposed.

LIVING IN A "REAL" WORLD

On the other side of the torn sky, in our valiant effort to deal with our very real disappointments, we mistakenly give in to the illusion of ultimate disappointment. We rightly want to face our difficulties head-on and not live in denial. We want to grow up and mature. We want to be able to accept the hand that we have been dealt and face our tragedies without sugarcoating them. But instead of facing our tragedies and allowing them to help us mature, we may grow cold and cynical or bitter and angry, creating a private dungeon of disillusionment. This is a pseudo-hell where we won't allow any good to interrupt our misery.

Equally an illusion, the so-called real world is a tight prison, and cynicism is the only currency that is exchanged. Instead of *growing* up, we find ourselves *giving* up. We wrongly think that the less we allow ourselves to feel life's disappointments and tragedies, the more mature we are and the more we are living in the real world.

Along come the philosophers to help us: "Detach from the world." And the talk-show hosts say, "Exploit the badness!" Some feminists would have us blame the men. All these voices say, "Life isn't as bad as you think it is—it's worse! Everybody is disappointed and messed up, and you shouldn't have expected anything different. Numb yourself with medication or any kind of religion, or figure out whose fault it is, but get over it. So your brother is a vegetarian transvestite who holds up convenience stores? You could have it a lot worse. Quit whining!"

The dungeon is like a cruel boot camp where we send our hearts to toughen them up. We want to separate those weak daddy's-girl dreams from the big, strong realities of *life*. The real world wants to confirm our deepest disappointments and serve up double helpings of what we've always been afraid of: Life is hard, so you'd better just face it now. You are alone. People are not good, and if they appear to be good, they're lying. Make your own way, and never depend on anyone else. Stop griping. Don't look for love; that reveals weakness. You don't need anything. God is not real, and dreams are for sissies or worse, for people out of touch with reality. Denial is anesthesia, and this is a world for tough people who never cry or bleed when they get cut.

There are no fake smiles here. In fact, there are no smiles at all in the dungeon. The so-called real world allows only an angry, clenched jaw and a fixed frown.

OUR OWN COMBINATION

If our overarching desire is a meaningful life still full of hopes and dreams, the illusion of a perfect world offers the equivalent of a diet soda to quench our deep thirst. The so-called real world serves up a double shot of Scotch whiskey. Neither is a satisfying choice.

If the "perfect" world is all there is, what happens when we grow too weary to pretend any longer?

If the "real" world is all there is, what will keep our hearts from dying in such an overwhelmingly brutal place?

Most of us know that both worlds are incomplete, but the choices are confusing. So we keep watching, listening, and consuming, trying to make sense of it all. Which world is the most real? Movies, songs, television, advertisements, life experiences—all add to the dilemma. They exercise their influence and pull and push. Believe this promise, or give up on that dream; let go of that faith, or hold on to this product. So we mix and match different elements from each world and end up with hearts looking like a crazy combination plate in a Mexican restaurant.

This is not a real solution either.

I will never forget the movie *Face Off* (John Travolta and Nicholas Cage) because of its disturbing combinations of good and evil. I sat watching a slow-motion scene of a violent shootout, but I heard no sound of gunfire from the automatic rifles and handguns. On the big screen I was seeing shooting and screaming and slow-mo images of bullets flying as incredible destruction took place, but all the while I, along with the other popcorn eaters, was hearing an incredibly beautiful rendition of "Somewhere over the Rainbow." Talk about confusing. I felt as if somebody had thrown "Somewhere over the Rainbow" up in the air and blasted it to bits in front of my eyes.

The illusion of a sugary sweet world looks perfectly positive, and the darkness of the so-called real world seems honestly negative, so we rationalize that together they will balance out each other. It doesn't work that way. Two halves will never make a whole when both are illusions. We have "fake it" on one side and "get over it" on the other. Pick your poison—saccharin or arsenic; it's death either way.

THE PRINCESS HEART

It wouldn't be so hard to have the heart of a princess if we lived in a fairy-tale world. The birds would wake us in the morning, we would have beautiful clothes laid out for us every day, a song would always be on our lips, and our good fairy godmother would be there to make certain our dreams always came true. Everyone would love us, and we would love everyone in return.

And in the real world it wouldn't be so hard to give up hope instead of struggling day after day to keep our dreams alive, because in this not-so-fairy-tale world, life is hard. We could openly acknowledge that the birds have gone south for the winter and probably died along the way. We could be cynical about everything, be mean to everyone. After all, we spend our days chained to the washing machine, covered in Cheerios, and on hold with the phone company. Why not admit we're miserable and create misery for everyone else?

Either way wouldn't be so bad, if we could pick our way and live accordingly. But we simply can't be satisfied by living exclusively in either world—both worlds are seductive and dangerous illusions and impossible to live in consistently. The difficulty in front of us is finding that place in-between—a place where we can cultivate the true heart of a princess, full of dreams, wonder, delight, and joy, right in the middle of this crazy, broken, hard-to-understand, disappointing world in which we live. That's a real challenge and one every woman in the world needs help to meet.

Whatever faith a woman has will play an important part in determining the way her heart will go, but only if it is a true faith, thought through and lived out. Faith in itself is by no means an antidote to detours. That's why Christian women are not immune to creating castles in the air or dungeons in the dark. In fact, faith can easily become the grandest illusion of all when it is merely used to support the false walls of a fake fairy-tale life. And equally dangerous is the real-world cynicism full of the ashes of burned-out religion that is impotent in the deeper workings of the heart.

So, what of the fairy-tale hopes we had? Are they just silly, romantic dreams of foolish schoolgirls? Made-up wishes of spoiled, privileged females who wanted more out of life than life could ever be expected to give? Or might they be the hidden, rarely confessed longings buried in the heart of every woman who walks the earth underneath a torn sky?

And what of those deep disappointments and sad realities we have had to face? Is that just the way this crummy life goes? Are they crystal-clear examples of why we should never get our hopes up again? Or could they be the harsh instruments that mine the depths of our character and reveal the valuable minerals of maturity?

What we want from life is so much bigger than one road or the other. Carefully, painstakingly we need to sift through each illusion to find the elements of truth.

Just when it seems we must settle for one of the two extremes, faith shows us another way. It illuminates a new place, an old place really—an invisible kingdom that can only be seen with the eyes of the heart. It's a place where our glimpses of the goodness of fairy tales (that seemed gone forever) can fit into a different view of reality. And it's where the realities of the so-called real world (that feel like hell on earth) are framed in a way that lightens the darkness and removes the cynicism. In this kingdom we can learn how to walk in the glass slipper on broken dreams. We can discover our princess hearts in a place that won't create an unrealistic ideal or collapse into fashionable cynicism.

In our normal, everyday world we have only seen hints of the power of this invisible kingdom, for it is a place entered only by faith. We have, however, heard the stories of a few who have gone before, whose lives changed the course of history. We marvel at the power of goodness when we read of the way Corrie Ten Boom's heart pushed up like a flower through the Nazi concrete sidewalk. And we recall how the fragrance of Mother Teresa's soul rose above the stench of India's sickness and despair. And we remember a group of firemen who showed courage that stood taller than the Twin Towers.

In time, a princess heart will begin to dream new dreams. Faith can rekindle old desires and create new hopes, replacing some of the old dreams we painfully watched die. But in the invisible kingdom we'll discover that the unseen dreams to come are bigger and more powerful than the small ones we've held so tightly in the past. We'll get new dreams of meaning and purpose that are much greater than whether or not the top of the TV gets dusted—dreams that are full of the kind of hope that is far stronger than despair.

What would it look like if we checked in with our three fairy-tale princesses, now living in the invisible kingdom? We just might find that . . .

Cinderella is not at the ball—she's at the ball game with her family, and she's loving life. "Hey batter, batter, batter . . . swing!" she yells from right field. She's got a baseball glove on her hand and a tiara on her head. The fairy godmother split, and most days Prince Charming isn't, but with the King of the universe helping her, she's doing just fine.

Sleeping Beauty is not sleeping—she's getting on with her life. At her desk, in her best business suit, she tells her assistant, "If a prince calls, take his number, and tell him I'll get back with him." She's got her pillow to support her back, not her illusions. She's no longer consumed by thoughts about earthly princes, because she has taken the hand of the Prince of Peace.

And Snow White is dressing down these days in jeans and a white tee-shirt. She's not pretending anymore, because she's given up on "perfect." She's still doing laundry for eight and wondering, "Sneezy? What is this on your shirt?" And these days there's still a whistle with the work, because she's discovered Christ, along with Clorox, for life's toughest stains.

Even though their lives are not what they might have planned, each of our heroines is quietly trusting that everything is going to work out just fine. Their dreams have matured, along with their faces. Each is living with the heart of a princess in our not-so-fairy-tale world.

There's a land that's far away,

But it can be reached on any day.

In this land live princesses fair,

And songs of merriment fill the air.

Anything is possible here.

Do you want a time of joy or fear?

Is it excitement that you want?

Like a kingdom to save or a dragon to taunt?

Or would you just like to have some fun?

Dance and play out in the sun?

Or maybe you'd like to be able to fly,

Soar for hours up in the sky.

What are your wishes? What are your dreams?

They can all come true in this land it seems.

"How do you get there?" you ask me now.

It's very simple; I'll tell you how!

Just sit back and fall into relaxation,

For this is the land of your imagination!

—KAYLA PARAMORE, *age 12*

CHAPTER TWO

Why Fairy Tales Matter

She was in the middle of a day that was just like the previous five days, that fell in the middle of a month exactly like the month before, that lined up in a year exactly like the last three years. She walked by the TV that had been on since 1989. She had a dull headache and a load of whites in one arm. She opened the door to the laundry room for exactly the one thousandth time, but instead of the familiar gaping mouths of the washer and dryer in front of her, there was a tiny open door revealing the first few steps leading to a winding staircase. She stared at the opening for a minute.

Would she drop all the socks and underwear on the floor and investigate the stairway? Or would she slam the laundry door closed and swallow a couple of Advil?

Long before I knew the stories were called fairy tales, I loved them. It would be years before I understood how fairy tales are different from other stories, but in my earliest memories, my heart soared when I heard the words "Once upon a time . . ."

Fairy tales are still very precious to me, but for far deeper reasons. Many of the tales provide direct glimpses into the way the world should have gone, delightfully confirming a deep suspicion that life should be different. As a friend of mine says, "The world should have been otherwise." Fairy tales verify this, and at the same time they reestablish hope that perhaps all is not lost and we just can't yet see the way life is going to turn out.

C. S. Lewis wrote that a good fairy tale will awaken "in us sensations that we have never had before, never anticipated having, as though we had broken out of our normal mode of consciousness and 'possessed joys not promised to our birth.' It gets under our skin, hits us at a level deeper than our thoughts or even our passions, troubles our oldest certainties till all questions are re-opened, and in general shocks us more fully awake than we are for most of our lives."

That is a tall order for a small story, but many of us have known this to be the case, especially with some of Lewis's writing.

Fairy tales provide an unexpected flash of hope that the brokenness and banality of this world is not all there is. They provide a counterintuitive look at the realities of everyday life. In short, they are wonderfully persistent, like children tugging at the sleeves of our hearts and pointing to a different world—a world that just might exist somewhere between the illusions of perfection and reality.

THE HIDDEN STRENGTH OF FAIRY TALES

Every fairy tale worth its salt (or its literary magic) creates a new world where things are different but true according to that world's alternative reality. For example, hobbits do not live in our world, but in the world of Middle Earth they live and breathe and laugh and sing. J. R. R. Tolkien would say that a good fairy-tale writer (he was one of the best) creates another world that our minds and hearts can enter and believe in fully while we are inside. A bad writer creates a world that we don't really believe. That forces us to sacrifice our belief and condescend to make-believe, in his words, "when trying to find what virtue we can in the work of art that has for us failed."

The worlds that Walt Disney created were magical for us as children but not big enough for us to grow up in, and so they failed us as adults. Walt's kingdoms were nice to visit when we were little, but as adults we hit our heads on the door trying to get back in. By contrast, the worlds other fairy-tale writers like Tolkien, C. S. Lewis, and George MacDonald created are larger, fully believable ones, in which we can come and go with ease. They are alternative worlds that can show us more about our own.

Well-known versions of *Cinderella* and *Sleeping Beauty* were written by a Frenchman named Charles

Perrault and the familiar version of *Snow White* by the Grimm brothers. Their stories didn't have the superficial, syrupy magic that Walt Disney added later for the big screen. Had those works stayed in their earlier forms, they might have retained their integrity with adults and better weathered the storms of life. But despite the Disney distortions, they still contain the necessary ingredients to make them classic fairy tales. And they still have much to teach us.

A good fairy tale has three important ingredients: recognition, adoration, and consolation. The details, the names, and the faces all can change—and do, delightfully. Each tale has its own unique characters and plot, and each draws us into the story in a different way. But a classic story will always contain those three important elements.

Recognition—The ugly duckling will be recognized as a swan. Snow White's beauty will not remain hidden forever. Cinderella will finally make it to the ball. In every fairy tale, whenever there is a princess, no amount of rags or dirt or envy from others can keep her from eventually being recognized. She will be found in the end.

Adoration—The princess will be loved. She may not know it at first. She may cry herself to sleep in utter loneliness, but trust this: Her prince is coming. Sleeping Beauty will not sleep forever. Cinderella will be loved in spite of that awful family. True love is on its way. The prince calls her his beloved, and nothing will stand in the way of his love.

Consolation—All will be well. There are a lot of obstacles in the story, and at first we can't see how it could possibly work out, but the darkness is going to part, and light is going to break through. The spell will be broken, the curse will be lifted, the sleeping princess will awaken, and the wicked queen will perish. There will be a glorious ending.

These three elements of story touch the deepest longings of a woman's heart: the desire to be known, the longing to be loved, and the yearning to see that all will be well. No wonder we love fairy tales. No wonder we cry when we watch a movie that skillfully weaves together these beautiful threads.

The good news is, these elements are rooted in the most wonderful tale of all time—the only one that is made more wonderful by the fact that it is true! It is the only story that has the power to change our lives. It is the greatest love story of all time. This is why fairy tales matter so much. As their little stories reflect the bigger story of the good news that is "the best news ever," once-hidden truths are illuminated. Like beacons of light across a stormy ocean, they can guide us safely to shores of belief. The tales stand in contradiction to the world we see around us and point to the world that is yet to come.

GLIMPSES INTO AN INVISIBLE KINGDOM

When a wardrobe becomes a doorway to another world, or a toad becomes a prince, it doesn't take us long to catch on to the fact that things are not always what they seem. When the beautiful sister is actually the ugly one, or when the queen who is supposed to be looking after the castle is wicked and deceitful, everything gets turned upside down.

The world of fairy tales sharply reveals that what we see around us is not all there is. There is more, much more. Fairy tales suggest and give glimpses of a very different, invisible kingdom—a world that lives between the illusions of the perfect and the real worlds. Not only is it in-between, it is upside down and inside out. In this kingdom the first are last. The hungry are the ones who will be fed, while those who say they are satisfied go hungry. The ordinary is really the extraordinary, and what others trumpet as extraordinary just might be as common as dirt.

Right now we see everything pretty dimly, like looking in a dirty mirror. We see things that shouldn't happen, and we don't understand why they do. Why is a little girl kidnapped from her home? How can an executive spend his employees' retirement money on his own lavish lifestyle? It's impossible not to be angry over things like this.

Fairy tales are like a pair of glasses—not the rose-colored kind that make everything look wonderful, but the kind that bring reality into focus. Like good bifocals, they help us discern the way the world really is up close, without losing the bigger picture of the way the world was intended to be. We must hold both views in our sights, the faraway and the closeup, at the same time.

AWAKENING OUR DEEPEST LONGINGS

A good fairy tale is always dangerous and subversive, because it awakens a yearning or a longing for something more than what is right in front of us. As C. S. Lewis said, fairy tales create a special kind of longing. It is not a longing that makes us despise what we have; it is the kind of longing that creates desire and makes us happy in the very fact of desiring. This desiring is good; it points us in the right direction. This yearning stretches us and lifts us toward what is right, ultimately toward God.

In the simplest of ways, fairy tales tunnel inside our hearts and spirits; they reach our tucked-away desires for love, truth, beauty, and joy; and they spring them free. Waking us up to dreaming again, they stoke our almost-burned-out desires—desires that are often easier to give up than to live with.

For example, few adult women would ever admit they desire to be a princess. This is partly because our grown-up hearts dismiss it so quickly as immature and impossible and partly because of the princesses' horrid reputation for being spoiled, demanding, and insecure. But tell a six-year-old girl, "You're a princess," and watch her whole countenance change. You've paid her the highest compliment there is. You've described with one phrase everything her little heart aspires to be. She doesn't know yet how strongly the world will come against her to steal that hope. She doesn't know yet how easy it will be to give it up, thinking she doesn't really need it. And she doesn't know yet if she relinquishes that desire, how hard it will be to get it back.

Start talking with any group of women about the idea that one day their princes will come, and watch their reactions. You'll get the scoffers and the angry women, who want to fight about men and their role in our lives, and you'll get the dreamy-eyed women, who live in a world of romance novels and soap operas and passively wait to be rescued. But mention the idea to your eighteen-year-old daughter that one day a man might recognize her for the true princess she is, and watch the sparkle in her eyes outshine the Hope diamond. She's not disappointed yet, nor have the delightful myths turned to saccharin—she's still aglow inside with the hope of real love.

Say the words "happily ever after" to six-year-olds, and they will believe in them, even though they don't have a clue yet what "happily ever after" means. Talk about it among women leaders or politicians, and you might be dismissed before the words come out. But mention it softly to the woman in the wheelchair facing the end of her life on earth, and the twinkle you see in her eyes could rival the North Star. We are most in touch with our deepest desires when we are closest to their fulfillment.

FANNING THE FLAME OF HOPE

Fairy tales offer hope. And hope, like nothing else in the world, inspires us and motivates us to keep going.

I once heard about an experiment with rats. A scientist put three rats in a tub of water to see how long they could swim before they drowned. The rats treaded water for about four hours, and two of them drowned. Before the third one went down, the scientist reached in and pulled him out. He dried the little fellow off and gave him a few days to rest up. A week or so later he conducted the experiment again. He put two rats in another tub of water, along with the one he'd rescued the week before. The little rats started treading water again, and unfortunately around that same four-hour mark the two new rats succumbed to fatigue and drowned. But the other rat, the one that had been rescued before, kept swimming. And swimming and swimming. That little rat swam for two days!

Hope is a powerful force!

Listed right up there with faith and love, it is in the top three strongest forces in the universe. But like the others, it is dependent on what it is connected to. Hope is not an engine; it's a hitch. Hope in hope doesn't work. Hope can't generate anything on its own. The strength of hope lies in what it hopes *in*—how strong it is depends on what it is connected to.

Along similar lines, we don't hope in the fairy tales themselves; we hope in the fulfillment of the longings they awaken in us. We don't hope that Cinderella is a true story; we hope that one day we will be recognized. We hope that Sleeping Beauty wakes up and that the curse is broken, because we long to wake up from the curse ourselves.

As they awaken our longings and reveal the invisible kingdom, fairy tales can help us keep going when we can't see what's ahead. So don't give up before the final act! Even though you are dressed in rags, laboring invisibly around people who don't seem to see you, you *are* a princess. Even though you think you have given up on love, it isn't over yet. Even though you can't see how any good could possibly come from the situation you are in, it may well turn out to be the very best thing of all. Hope says don't just look with your eyes, look with your heart.

All of these elements are why we love fairy tales, why we loved them as girls and then as teenagers. And now that we are women, they have never been more important to our hearts. We are drawn to these elements the way we are drawn to a hearth with a warm fire when we are cold. They thaw our deepest longings.

These three ingredients of fairy tales—recognition, adoration, and consolation—are the strong desires of a princess heart. By delving into the truth and reawakening the hope of these elements, we can keep wonder and passion alive. Our hearts will dream bigger dreams than whatever we see pictured on the cover of the latest magazine. Our hearts will stay soft even when everything around us is so hard to bear. These simple elements are the gold that remains in the bottom of our hearts as we sift through the river of pain, picking out the rocks of disappointment.

As we discover parts of the invisible kingdom that live in the worlds of fairy tales, we will discover parts of our hearts too. Because somewhere between the *perfect* world, and the so-called *real* world, there is a world that is infinitely more real than our own. As we take this journey together, we might find ourselves asking the same question Lucy asked in The Chronicles of Narnia, "Will you tell us how to get into your kingdom from our world?"

She blinked a few times, and the door was still there. It was time for a change. Her heart pounded with excitement. She skipped the Advil, dropped the socks and underwear on the floor, and headed for the stairway . . .

CHAPTER THREE

Castles in the Air

$\mathcal{T}$here is a wedding this afternoon in the English country manor where I am staying. I'm tucked up in my room writing, but from my window I can see all the activity below. The musicians and caterers showed up hours ago, and now the family is excitedly arriving. Exhilaration fills the whole manor, and it is bustling with joy. The harpist—yes, a harpist—is playing on the grass, and through my open window I feel as though I have taken my place on the lawn among the honored guests. No one knows me, but we are one in our longing for a splendid day. I feel a few butterflies in my own stomach. I find myself praying for them. My spirit is sunning in the happiness and the holiness of what I hope will be one of the most special days of their lives.

As I watch, the bride arrives in an old 1960s white Rolls Royce. What an entrance! As she steps from the car, I hardly notice her white gown, because she is clothed far more beautifully in her hopes and dreams.

All eyes are on her—she is the only one who matters, but not because she has stamped her foot and insisted on it. Love has pushed her into the center of attention on this day. Everyone close to her wants her to begin this new life in the most wonderful way possible.

A bride on her wedding day is the closest thing to a princess in a fairy tale that we experience in our everyday world. A wedding creates the most beautiful atmosphere possible. Just walking into a church or a beautiful garden decorated for a wedding can stir us, awakening deep longings not only for the bride and the groom, but for all who have gathered to witness the ceremony. A marriage, like a fairy tale, is a celebration of wonderful things about life and love. The greenery of the plants and flowers, the family and friends, the symbolism of the candles and rings, the imagery of the bride in white—all aspects point to the hope of a new life full of love and great joy.

It is right that we should desire to live in a world full of love. Our hopes to have beautiful homes and lovely gardens are neither bad nor wrong. Our longings for happy endings are good. All these hungers remind us that our hearts are homesick for a better world—a world that runs the way it is supposed to, a world not ruined by sin. For it is sin, or the way the world has gone wrong, that is the real wrong—not our desires, not our dreams, not our longings.

TROUBLE IN PARADISE

Paul Marshall writes this in *Heaven Is Not My Home:*

> Sin is not the story; it is the blight on the story. Sin distorts everything, perverts everything, and corrupts everything. It is not sin that makes us bear children, but it is sin that makes childbearing painful. It is not sin that attracts men and women, but it is sin that fills our relations with control and suspicions. It is not sin that makes music, but it is sin that fills our songs with vanity and lust. It is not sin that makes us construct cities and towers, but it is sin that makes those towers symbols of pride and power. It is not sin that calls human beings to live and love, to make music and art, to work and create, to plant and to harvest, to play and dance. But it is sin that undercuts and perverts them all.
>
> Sin does not create things. It has no originality, no creativity, no being in itself. Sin lives off that which is good. It is a parasite, feeding greedily on the goodness of what God has made.

The goodness of what God has made and the hints of the way the world *should* have gone are evident everywhere. We see it so clearly when we are captivated by nature's raw beauty. We notice it when we are playing or throwing our heads back in laughter. We experience it when we are dancing or reading poetry.

We taste it when we sit down to a great meal. And we feel it most keenly when we love. There is so much to taste and see and enjoy and feel in the lives God has given us.

But alas, as wonderful as it all is, it still falls short. Beauty is marred, the laughter ends, the dance is over, nature changes, and love wounds. Nothing lasts. Even the dusk is poignant in its own way. Everything around us has been touched by sin, and even the best things are affected.

So it is with truth. Scripture cautions us, because we "suppress the truth in unrighteousness." We stifle the natural voice and direction of truth, and we twist it to fit our wills and our ways. But even the sinful way we hold truth doesn't make it less true. The truth remains the truth. We may take good things and pervert them, but that doesn't mean they are not good. It means that what we've done with them isn't good, like eating so much Healthy Choice ice cream that it's no longer a healthy choice.

We often begin by holding the gold (the nuggets of truth hidden in fairy tales) and end up clutching it so tightly it becomes a disfigured, misshapen image. This is the way we start to build castles in the air. We take good gifts, greedily cling to them, and even worship them, ignoring the Giver of these gifts. This does not create a princess heart. It does just the opposite—it becomes idolatry that will deform our hearts and make them vulnerable.

THE TELLTALE TEMPTATIONS

Temptation is a suggested short cut to the realization of the highest at which I aim—not towards what I understand as evil, but towards what I understand as good.

—OSWALD CHAMBERS

When we are accused of living in a world of denial or of fairy-tale thinking, it's pretty safe to say we went there for good reasons. We want the good stuff. Every woman I know is trying to make her life better in some way—with better communication with her husband, better lawn care for the yard, a better school system for the kids. We want life to get better every day. We were made for the things we find in fairy-tale worlds. It's hard for us to keep our heads out of the clouds when our hearts so badly want to live there.

We were made for faith, hope, and love. But, again, sin corrupts, and as we try to hold the truth with our sin-stained hands, we can start to worship faith, hope, and love themselves, instead of the God who made them. Then we end up with faith in faith or with hope in hope or in love with love, which are all ridiculous when you think about them. Putting our faith in faith, or in mere positive thinking, robs power and strength from faith, if there is no real God behind it. Hope is only as strong as that in which it hopes. And falling in love with love will put us on a perpetual hamster wheel of romance that will never bring us closer to the real thing.

Christian women are often accused of building castles in the air. The truth is, it's a temptation for every woman, no matter her spiritual inclinations. Yes, faith can give a nudge to illusions, but plenty of women can live in fantasy worlds with no help from religion. Turn on any soap opera in the afternoon, and see the women of daytime drama floating on a raft of pretense, completely adrift from reality. Magazines of self-help and home decorating have created a church all their own. With wreaths and hot glue and cheap therapeutic advice, women worship by the millions. Take a stroll down Rodeo Drive in Beverly Hills and spot woman after woman climbing strenuously to the top of the "Best Dressed" ivory tower. One glance at *People* magazine will reveal the lavish attempts to create a fairy-tale wedding for the latest superstar. Women everywhere are pulling out all the stops and pursuing like crazy a make-believe world.

The nuggets of true gold that we gleaned from fairy tales—recognition, adoration, and consolation—also provide the breeding ground for great temptations. If we take shortcuts toward our great desires, we run the risk of getting lost in the woods. The good things we seek can become isolated from their roots and their larger truths, and we could end up with castles in the air. In *The Weight of Glory,* C. S. Lewis gives a stern warning about the way we hold these things, saying that they are

. . . good images of what we really desire; but if they are mistaken for the thing itself they turn into dumb idols, breaking the hearts of their worshippers. For they are not the thing itself; they are only the scent of a flower we have not found, the echo of a tune we have not heard, news from a country we have not yet visited. Do you think I am trying to weave a spell? Perhaps I am; but remember your fairy tales. Spells are used for breaking enchantments as well as for inducing them.

THE DISTORTION OF RECOGNITION

It's a thrilling point in every fairy tale: The obstacle that has been obscuring the view of everyone is removed, and the princess is seen as having her true worth and value.

Don't underestimate this powerful desire—it flickers in all of us. Most women labor invisibly, day after day. The majority of things we do no one sees or acknowledges, but the moment someone does see or notice is absolute heaven. We feel as though a veil has been lifted. To be valued and esteemed is one of our deepest longings. We hunger to be known and recognized for who we are—or more honestly, for who we *hope* we are.

Recognition is right. And I don't just mean recognition for accomplishments or deeds, although that is certainly part of it. The greater recognition is in worth and value apart from any deeds, the sturdy confirmation that we are worth more than the sum total of what we accomplish in this life. Like every unknown princess in a fairy tale, we long for our day of recognition.

However, being a princess in the eyes of God doesn't move us toward a princess heart if we worship recognition over worshiping the One who recognizes. In the absence of truly worshiping the King who names us, we are fully capable of fashioning that precious piece of beautiful gold he offers into a little statuette that looks a lot like us. What a difference there is between trying to be a princess and trusting that God has named us a princess. The first will push us toward an unrealistic view of life and an unchecked self-centeredness. The other one will humble our hearts and deepen our faith.

In fact, even the name *princess* creates confusion, as we will see more fully later. Princesses in the past were not always on their best behavior. Because we don't have royalty in America, we've tried to recreate the princess role over the years in ways that don't even come close. Between Hollywood starlets and pop music divas, we have few examples that define what a true princess looks like, much less paragons of a princess heart.

If a woman worships worth, she must prove her worth over and over; she cannot accept it as a gift. When we worship the idol of recognition—how others see us, what we look like, how well we perform—we are finding ways to pay homage to ourselves. We are attempting to prove to the world by all we do and all we have that our lives matter. It's all about *us*.

You can see this idolatry anywhere you find women holding to an unreal standard of perfection. It's obvious in workouts, wardrobes, and weddings, in furniture, fingernails, and family. Many women are striving to be the best—not the best they can be—the best, period. They have made themselves into idols.

Thinking we can live in the perfect world is perfect in one simple way: It's the *perfect lie*. It's perfect because we want to believe it so badly that it doesn't take much to sell us on it.

MARTHA, MARTHA, MARTHA

Martha Stewart didn't sell housewares or linens or even canapés. She peddled the illusion of a perfect life. And if her company's bottom line was an accurate indication, we all wanted to buy it. We bought towels and dishes; we bought wreaths made from homegrown vines. We read her magazine, watched her programs, and invested in our own hot glue guns. We wanted to be Martha. But like everything else that sets itself up too high, it topples. And so did Martha. There were many before her, and it won't take long for another to rise in her place.

It's almost as if we thought Martha was a savior— that somehow she could show us the way to find recognition in a *perfect* world. We held hope in our hearts that if we did things exactly as she did, she would lead us to a better life. But then our husbands didn't notice the new changes, and our mothers still criticized the wreaths, and the kids wiped bicycle grease on the towels and put cat food in the new dishes. No recognition there. Instead of getting what we wanted from Martha, we felt let down and disappointed. We felt even more betrayed by the amount of money she made selling us hope.

The truth is, when we are worshiping recognition, we just use our idols to confirm or deny what we already believe is true about ourselves. But there is a law of diminishing returns: The more we get, the more we want. We love our idols when they come through for us, but when they fall off their pedestals and smash into a million pieces, we despise them. If we feel insecure before we buy dishes, we will feel insecure after. If we aren't sure how our husband feels about us, and we buy sexy lingerie to spice up a special evening, chances are good we still won't be so sure about him the morning after. Why? Because we are using things, and possibly even people, to confirm or deny what we believe or what we fear is true about ourselves.

The battle is in us, because the sin is in us. We have great value; that is not in dispute. But we didn't achieve or create that value—we were *given* that value. God noticed us before we accomplished anything. Yet if we worship that value or believe that we created it, or if we try to increase it in illegitimate ways, we are involved in idolatry. And idolatry is cruel slavery that leads to more misery and increased insecurity.

However, being recognized for nothing you've done

on your own—this changes everything. Somehow you begin to realize that the King has seen you and named you and given you a worth and value that is not of yourself. Trusting in this truth is the one sure way to escape an insatiable craving for recognition. And it is essential to discovering a princess heart.

THE DISTORTION OF ADORATION

The second piece of gold we can see, thanks to our awakening from the fairy tales, is the truth that we were made for love. Love is right. It is the strongest of all human emotions. Love is the ultimate invitation to life. Always beckoning, love calls to us and says, "Join me— you were not meant to be alone." Life sends us a personal invitation through love, and our hearts quickly RSVP.

If we grew up in good families, it was love that first drew us out of our rooms. Gathering around the kitchen for laughter and conversation, we wanted to be wherever love was. I can remember lying in my bed at 7:30 at night, wondering how they could have so much fun without me. I wanted to be out there.

As we made friends, love drew us out of our shells. Walking to school with others we could talk to made going to school better. Finding another person who liked the same things we liked made us brave and confident. Laughing in the lunchroom over the same boys knit our hearts in joyous camaraderie.

And if we found a heart for companionship, it was

love that drew us out of ourselves. Giving of yourself to another person is officially celebrating the best of what it means to be human. That is when love reveals its true strength—it becomes strongest when it is given away.

Love is a brush in your hand that makes you an artist, painting colors you had only dreamed of. It is a pen that makes you a writer, flowing with words you could never have imagined. Talk to parents on the day their baby is born about their dreams for the future. Ask a couple on their wedding day to describe the sunset they're watching. The wonderful feelings that accompany love are strong and right and real.

However, the great temptation we face with love is to distort its gold into a little heart-shaped charm. Women become addicted to the feelings of love, and they fall in love with love. Watching love and romance on the big screen, we can begin to worship love's feelings rather than the Giver of all love.

MARVELOUS MEG

For a number of years, Meg Ryan was the poster woman for romantic comedies, which I absolutely love—most of the time. The good ones are modern-day fairy tales, and they inspire and delight me. The bad ones are like falling into cotton candy for a couple of hours—you're sticky for a long time afterward. But even the good ones must be held in our hearts in the right way, or we can miss the joy of real love, for which we were made, and end up in the ditch of sentimentality. Finding that, instead of holding the truth, we are treasuring the trite.

When we see Meg Ryan and Tom Hanks meet on the screen, our stomachs do flip-flops, our hearts become acrobats. I would never dismiss that; I want to celebrate it. The greatest pulse quickeners and spirit-soaring stories of all times are love stories. But the true greats are not sentimental romantic comedies; they are portraits of love incarnate. The real gymnastics of the heart should never be confused with the cheap tricks of the World Wrestling Federation. If we make love an idol, we end up with a showy, sappy, sloppy emotion that is simply not strong enough for real life.

Sentimentality might help a bad hair day, but for the deeper issues of life, it falls miserably short. If you see a movie after being diagnosed with cancer, you need more than a good feeling that lasts about as long as a nice latte. Sentimentality never satisfies. It's a mile wide and an inch deep.

Take this quick quiz:

HOW SENTIMENTAL ARE YOU?

1. **How often do you cry at movies?**
   _____ Never. I'd have to pluck a nose hair.
   _____ Once in a while when someone dies.
   _____ Every movie has something sad.
   _____ Why don't they just sell tissues at the theater?

2. **How many romantic comedies have you seen?**

_____ Meg Ryan? Is she that blond girl?

_____ One, and I took medication immediately following.

_____ Only the ones I can trick someone into seeing with me.

_____ Seen or own?

3. **How often do you watch programs with angels in them?**

_____ Never.

_____ I saw a few when my mother was visiting.

_____ I enjoy watching angels after the evening news.

_____ We watch them as a group and then have our weekly Bible study.

4. **How many things in your home have ruffles on them?**

_____ None. I don't like those kinds of potato chips.

_____ I have one throw pillow that was a wedding gift.

_____ Twelve things, not including the dog's collar.

_____ What's wrong with ruffles? Are you making fun of me?

5. How many romance novels have you read?

_____ None since high school.

_____ I started one in a weak moment but never finished it.

_____ In a week? Or in a day?

_____ What's wrong with romance novels?

_____ Okay, I'm starting to see a pattern.

Feeling good is simply not enough for a woman's heart. If we can't distinguish between love and sentimentality, then when sentimentality fails us—and it will—we'll blame love. Not only is that devastating; it's wrong. If we decide that love isn't worth it or love isn't true, we run the risk of giving up on love. That's far different from recognizing what is and what isn't love to begin with, so that in the future we can put our weight down on the real thing.

Sentimentality will not carry us through the hard times in our lives, but real love will. That is why we must be ruthless when we look at our desire for adoration and talk about longings like "someday your prince will come" (we'll talk more about him later). These can so easily be distorted and lead us to the idolatry of love and romance. Romance will not be strong enough to survive an affair, but real love can. Living in a world of phony novels, taping our favorite daytime dramas every day, or even filling our homes with paintings of light will not do the trick. Each obscures our view of real adoration. All the substitutes give the same short-term feel-good, like a sugar high. And when the feel-good goes away, only the headache remains.

But let romance give way to reality, let love find its anchor in the commitment and sacrifice that God has demonstrated, and there is no sediment of sentiment. This is the love that is stronger than death. This is the love that gives all other loves their depth of meaning and passion. This is the love that is hotter than any blazing fire. This is the love that burns the dross of distortion away from the gold of real adoration. This is the love that forges a princess heart.

THE DISTORTION OF CONSOLATION

She paints her world in yellow and green,
covering over the gray,
'cause life's demands are hard to understand,
so Alice stays lost in her Wonderland.
—WAYNE KIRKPATRICK

The third piece of gold we are awakened to in fairy tales is the euphoric joy of the happy ending. It's gotten a bum rap from the words "happily ever after," which usually characterize the ending of classic tales. Tolkien dismisses these words as nothing more than a device, not an actual description of events. They are simply a way to stop a story that in reality would continue on and on without them. They are like a frame around a photo. You don't confuse the frame with the photo; it is only the border.

Our desire for consolation is profoundly deep. We experience it as relief when we encounter the wonderful turn at the point in the story, in which it seems all will be lost. It is a dramatic change for good that sweeps in like an unexpected grace, taking our breath away and lifting our spirits to new heights. We realize then how strongly we were hoping. Sometimes it is so powerful that we weep with joy. No fairy tale is complete without this turn. And in the best fairy tale of all we know that God is keeping an eye on the time and that he will give us the grandest happily ever after we can imagine.

However, we can also fashion this piece of gold into an idol when we trust the happy ending more than we trust the Author of the play. We make an idol that looks like a great big cheerful bow. We paste it on the end of every story, of every life, of every day, or even every sentence, whether the Author wants it there or not. We can distort "happily ever after" to mean that everything will have a happy ending whether or not it really does.

Women are great at writing a happy ending for every story. Part of this is a gift and faith, but another part is sin, and it often amazes me how quickly we go to the sinful part. We don't want to live unsettled by things we don't understand, so we simplify them to absurdity. We make up explanations for why things happen to help ourselves feel better, but our explanations are transparently thin. Scratch the surface, and you have nothing real on which to put your confidence.

We easily hurt others by pasting those bows on their

stories. Just listen to conversations between women at the office water cooler, or at their kids' preschool. You'll find one woman who hasn't quite finished her sorrow-filled tale of survival after losing her husband to leukemia and another woman who interrupts, "Well, you know, *Godisworkingallthingstogetherforgood*."

Of course we *do* believe that ultimately God is bringing all of the difficulties in our lives together in a way that has meaning and purpose, but we cannot presume to understand it all or explain it away so easily. The difference between trusting that there is an ultimate happy ending and making an idol of that ending lies in our willingness to let it be a mystery of God's timing and not of our choosing. We have to stand in the complexity of all that God is working on, not just in the simple part we can see for ourselves. We must relinquish our arrogance and presumption that we have figured out God's plan.

The woman who makes the happy ending an idol finds that life in the *real* world is far too complicated for her to abandon her castle in the air. The black and white of good and evil are very distinct where she resides, and there is just no room for gray. All the colors are bright and pretty, and the whites always get washed separately from the darks. Every problem has a simple solution, and every wrinkle can be pressed out. Every boo-boo gets a quick kiss, and the little cuts and scrapes will all be better soon.

It is true that the demands of living in a complex

world are overwhelming at times. From unclear relationship difficulties to unfathomable global issues, life is terribly hard to understand. But to go around putting cartoon Band-Aids on the gaping wounds of the world is denial. There is nothing more unattractive than a happy face that has been pasted over a grimace of pain.

A CHRISTMAS LETTER FROM ALICE IN WONDERLAND

Everything runs right on time,
years of practice and design,
spit and polish 'til it shines,
He thinks he'll keep her.
—MARY CHAPIN CARPENTER

You open the red envelope, and there they are again, all dressed in Christmas sweaters this year, even the family spaniel. Meet the holiday greeting card clan smiling for the camera. That's Alice in the middle, keeping everything together. Her son, Chris didn't want to wear a tie under his sweater and swore when she told him he had to. Jerry, her husband, was twenty minutes late for the sitting. When the photographer suggested they go ahead for a few shots without Dad, Martin—the middle boy said, "No problem, we always do."

A few days ago she got the pictures back, and she sat down to write the letter that would accompany the smiling family photo. She'd have to lie again, but she would never call it that. She'd just laugh sweetly and cover for Jerry, who is working way too much. She'd make the kids' grades and achievements *slightly* better than they really are. And when it was all written and postmarked, she'd quietly wonder what she really does with her life.

If everything already feels like it's falling apart, wouldn't telling the truth just make it worse? Her marriage is limping along, but if she confronted Jerry, it might be the end. She just can't stop being "the good girl." She knows how to do the right thing, even if it involves pretending. But she can't face the problem, because it's too complicated. So, instead, she just keeps patching everything with sugary mortar, hoping for the best.

Her letter would be comical if it weren't so sad. She gets worse and worse every Christmas. She alternates between being angry with herself for not telling the truth and feeling overwhelming sorrow for the way things have turned out. On most days she doesn't let herself feel much of anything.

Alice is the undisputed workhorse of the church and school. She volunteers more than anyone else, drives the carpool more than her share, and wipes the noses in the nursery. But lately it's been her own nose, more than any of the kids' she looks after.

Jerry works five nights a week. Never mind about his secretary Stephanie and the unexplained expenses—Alice won't let herself think about that right now. "He's a good man," she writes, as she struggles to think of something else nice to say about him. "We're all really proud of him and the way he's advancing at work. We think he'll be president of the company soon." She draws a smiley face after her words. Jerry hasn't told Alice that he loves her once in the last two years, but she pretends that it doesn't really matter.

Chris, her oldest, now seventeen, has enormous mood swings. She can't bring herself to think it might be drugs, even though the police have brought him home twice. She and Chris can't have a ten-minute conversation, but she simply assumes that she's a little out of touch with his generation. She writes, "He's really becoming quite a man," even though all she really wants from him is to make up his bed, turn down his music, and be nice to girls. He can't stand her, but she writes, "We're learning a lot about how to live with a teenager . . ."

Martin is her tender-hearted piano player—just fourteen and flunking algebra. She's gotten him a tutor, but he refuses to try, preferring instead the solitude of his own room and his melancholy nature. She wishes he would smile sometimes, but she has no idea why he doesn't. She's dreaming again when she writes, "Martin is showing great promise this year, and we think he might go to medical school . . ."

Sarah is Daddy's little girl—but wearing things that make her mother wince. Every day is a battle. "Sarah is coming into her own and blossoming right in front of us. She has wonderful fashion sense, and, like me, she loves to shop." She was sent home from school last month for being dressed inappropriately. She was wearing something she had borrowed from her friend Jennifer, which she changed into on the way to school.

Next week Alice's life will come crumbling down. Her husband will announce he is leaving, and her son will be kicked out of school. Martin will take everything the hardest, and Sarah will be pregnant in a year's time. What will she write in next year's letter?

OUR UNFINISHED STORIES

A woman has great capacity, God-given I believe, to ignore pain and allow love to cover a multitude of sins. But when she holds to the illusion that everything is just fine when it so clearly is not, she has stepped into a dreamlike world of pretense. She is refusing to cooperate with a life unwilling to cooperate with her, preferring instead to live in Wonderland. Alice's story may yet have a good ending. Much will depend on her willingness to give up her controlling idolatry of making everything happy on the surface.

We are never promised that *everything* will have a happy ending. We are not even promised that we will live to see all the joyous turns we long for. Our sons may not give up their drugs, our neighbors might not recover from cancer, but we have been given the promise that we haven't seen the ending yet. We have been given the hope that what we see is not the sum of all that is happening and the glorious revelation that the Author isn't finished yet. So we don't put our trust only in the happy ending; we put our trust in the Author of the happy ending. This is the way out of the distorted view we have of ultimate consolation. It is the hope of the princess heart.

It's easy to confuse the longing for the ultimate happy ending with the illusion of that temporary "happily ever after." We were created to be loved, so it's understandable that we could fall in love with love. And it is our God-given desire to be recognized that tempts us to seek our own recognition. But faith, like a fairy tale, creates wonder, never illusion. It inspires and delights; it doesn't deny and sugarcoat. We long to live in the truths *revealed* by fairy tales, not in the illusion of living the fairy tales themselves. The truths offer freedom and the illusion pure slavery.

The tables are always set beautifully in castles in the air, but look closer to see the paint is peeling badly. Alice is leading the way to denial, Meg is pushing us toward sentimentality, and Martha is cracking the whip of perfectionism—each touching something in us that is very real: our deepest desires.

It would be nice to blame Martha and Meg and Alice for the way they have led us astray, but it's not their fault. The illusions are seductive on their own, because they call out to the deepest places within us. But allowing those desires to become idols of worship, instead of altars of sacrifice, will indeed break our hearts. Instead of the life we wanted, we get a life as thin as a temporary Hollywood facade. And like the best in Tinseltown, it's a very expensive front—costly in more ways than one.

Isn't it time we came down from our castles in the air?

How will she keep a princess heart in a not-so-fairy-tale world? Will she breathlessly chase after the world's recognition by seeking to impress everyone? Can she quietly trust that God has called her a princess? Will she give in to entitlement thinking and become demanding and spoiled? Can she believe with all her heart in the power of real love without giving in to sentimentalism that never satisfies? Can she trust in the God of history, who promises that one day "all will be well," or must she bear the weight of pretending it is already that way every day?

CHAPTER FOUR

Dungeons in the Dark

Her heart aches with all the longings it holds. It is forever yearning and wrestling with hungers that simply won't be satisfied. But she doesn't know that's why she can't find her way. So she keeps packing, cramming, stuffing round pegs into the very square hole of her heart, creating deeper and deeper disappointments. She needs someone to tell her she is not wrong for hoping and that her desires are not too big but too small. But no one has, so she thinks something is terribly wrong with her. She doesn't know she's halfway to a princess heart.

It was a magnificent sunny afternoon, which in England is a glorious event in itself. I was visiting Leeds, the loveliest castle in the world, surrounded by happy people strolling and picnicking. But right in front of me a little boy was crying. I mean wailing. He was about seven, and he wanted to ride the train around the castle. Unfortunately there wasn't enough room for the boy's family, so they had to walk, which is how I ended up behind them.

His father tried to console him, saying, "Next time, son."

But the little boy was smarter than that. "There won't be a next time," he sniffled through his tears.

His mother said, "Who wants to ride that old train anyway?"

That brought a new wave of sadness. *"I* do," he cried. *"I* want to ride the traaaaiiinnn!"

A tiny part of me was annoyed that the soundtrack of a screaming child was accompanying my visit to the castle. But my truer heart wanted to take his little face in my hands and say, "I'm sorry, I'm *so* sorry." There was nothing else to say. Sometimes there just isn't enough room on the train. His father was telling him gently, "Let it go." And by saying, "Who wants to ride that old train?" his mother was teaching him, *Just act as if you didn't really want to anyway.*

Neither response was satisfying to the child. In fact, both responses just made him cry harder. And in a strange way, I could feel the pain in his tears. His heart is just like mine. While it's not trains anymore, there are heartbreaking disappointments in my life that are difficult to face. Like that little boy, I wonder what I'm supposed to do with my heart.

DISAPPOINTMENT MANAGEMENT
AND LONGING LOBOTOMIES

*Thoreau wrote that most men lead lives
of quiet desperation.
I say that women do too; we're just not so quiet about it.*

Disappointments are inevitable; life breaks our hearts. So how do we keep our hearts from learning the wrong lessons from those disappointments? In the last chapter, we looked at the difficulties created when we make idols of good things. Putting too much belief in one particular part of the truth distorts that truth. But turn the gold coin over and notice the flip side. Disbelief. Un-belief.

Not putting enough belief in the truth also distorts it. If we define truth only by what we can see, feel, and touch, we limit our belief out of fear and pain, which creates an equally devastating distortion. When we do this, rather than elevating the truths in the fairy tales into idolatry, we subjugate them to the realm of pathology. We see them as a disease—something wrong in our hearts that needs to be removed or an illness from which we need to recover.

In simple terms, we are trying to cure our hearts from hoping.

Fairy tales don't have to work at inspiration or comfort—these wonderful qualities emanate through the pores of the stories. And our hearts don't make a decision to be glad when the recognition occurs. It's a natural response. When the prince finds the princess, we don't think about why adoration makes sense; we dance. And when the ending takes its glorious turn, we don't analyze why consolation is so important to us. We just silently wipe away the tears.

You don't find hope; it finds you. But hope is a double-edged sword. While it's elevating and inspiring, after a few too many disappointments, we aren't so sure we want our hopes raised anymore. When the fairy tales stir up hope, and our hungry hearts respond, if life doesn't come through, we get out of sorts with hope. Perhaps we're even angry with the fairy tales for letting us down. We missed the ending we wanted. Where was the detour sign? Snow White to the left—Black Misery to the right? No one gave us a choice. It would have been better never to hope for anything.

Have you given up hope? Try taking this little quiz to discover the shade of your jade:

Happily ever after is a myth . . .
____ Only during my period.
____ Almost every day.
____ Since 1941.

Someday my prince will come . . .
____ About 5:30, after work.
____ He got lost on the way and wouldn't ask for

directions.

____ Yep, he came, and now he's in the other room, watching TV.

If there were a glass slipper . . .

____ I would try it on for fun.

____ I would assume it doesn't come in my size.

____ I would fill it with rocks and plants and make a terrarium.

My biggest dream is . . .

____ A richer life.

____ More money than bills.

____ A good night's sleep.

If seven dwarfs showed up on my doorstep, I might . . .

____ Invite them in for tea.

____ Act like I don't speak English.

____ Call the exterminator.

(Hint: if you chose the last option every time, please keep reading.)

When I think of all the longings that are unfulfilled for most women, when I think of all the things that never come to completion for many of us, it breaks my heart. The great sadness of our lives is recognizing all of the things that are left incomplete and unfulfilled on this earth.

Many of these will remain unresolved until heaven,

but that doesn't mean we deny them or kill them. With so many heartbreaks and so much sin in the world, our answer has been to put our hearts through a training course in "disappointment management," which ultimately acts like a longing lobotomy. A cautious voice says, "Don't get your hopes up." The voice doesn't go away until our desires are quietly tamed and eventually hope is altogether removed.

Simone Weil warns, "The greatest danger is that the soul should persuade itself it is not hungry." Our longings are boundless. That's how we were made. Our hearts are not small. Our desires are not predictable. We cannot be figured out easily. There will always be more to women than anyone can imagine or calculate or expect or predict. And God loves that about us. He's not embarrassed by that or worried because we're so complicated. He welcomes our deepest hungers and our strongest questions.

Like most people, we want to be smart and *real-world* minded. We don't want to be Pollyannas in other people's eyes. We want to stand on the side of truth and justice and face the dark side bravely. And this is right. But the danger, as we seek to understand evil, is that our hearts give way. We spiral down from under-standing it in context to a resigned acceptance of it. We descend from sadness over the ways things have gone awry to anger that we ever hoped the world would deliver anything different. Before we know it, we've lost our footing and along with it wonder, awe, imagination, nobility, beauty, and grace. We find ourselves sliding down the hillside of our hearts to become casualties of the fashionable (and understandable) cynicism that pervades our culture.

Fairy tales can help. They have the uncanny ability to bring to the surface our submerged disappointments. Cut loose by a good story, they can bob around, revealing our cynicism, our anger, or the cruel way we've treated our dreams. Isn't it surprising how often we are mean to our own hearts for hoping? We want to teach ourselves a lesson for wanting too much and for getting our hopes up yet again. We flog and whip ourselves for doing what comes naturally in the face of disappointment—longing for something better. We wrongly believe that we would rather inflict pain now than open ourselves up to that kind of hurt again.

A VISIT TO THE DUNGEON OF WARWICK CASTLE

I park the car in a space way too small for it, so tiny that I have to lose weight to get out. That's not all bad, because it's pouring down rain again, so I have time. When it slacks off to a steady deluge, I suck in my stomach, grab my notebook, camera, and jean jacket, and set out on the footpath. After running—okay walking fast—for about a mile, I start to wonder if I'm heading in the right direction. It seems very far, but twenty yards is too far when you're running in the rain. I guess you can't exactly drive up to the front door of a castle and ring the bell.

The trees form a ceiling of branches above my head. Due to the fog and rain and way too many scary movies, the lower branches seem like arms that might reach out and grab me at any moment. I hear a scream, and I almost scream. It takes me a minute (and about seven rapid heartbeats) to identify what shrieked—a peacock. I find it odd that a bird so beautiful makes such a hideous sound.

I look up, after being lost in my peacock thoughts, to catch my first glimpse of Warwick Castle. It's enormous. I can't be too far from the entrance, and it hurts my neck to look up that high. It's a fortress. Forget what I said about the front door; you wouldn't want to ring the bell if there was one. This is a real castle. I'm not in Santa Monica anymore. It is imposing, formidable, and more than a little ominous.

I cross over the huge drawbridge with its iron spikes pointing down at me, and I'm speechless. But I'm alone, so it doesn't make any difference. Suddenly I'm jerked back to the present by more shrieks, but this time from school kids. They are everywhere, running around this enormous castle with their tiny little backpacks and knee-socks. There is canned Renaissance music playing and a tour guide dressed up as an archer, awkwardly holding an umbrella. All sorts of medieval games are set up in tents around the outside of the castle. In the pouring rain, the kids are playing Skee-Ball, which I seriously doubt they did in medieval times.

I duck under the awning of the ticket booth,

request one adult pass, and am ushered through the gate into a little courtyard of food and gifts. It takes something away from the big, dark castle when you can buy a cappuccino right in front of the dungeon. I like coffee but not necessarily while I'm standing over the pit of despair. Despite all the commercialism (I'm sure it's not cheap to keep a fortress up and running these days), I close my eyes. Alone in the courtyard with more than a thousand years of history, I try to imagine what it must have been like to live in Warwick Castle.

Beginning the tour, I stop first at the dungeon and stand for a long time in the small space. Enormous cold stones make up the floor and walls. Candles are lit for the visitors so we don't run into anything, but I'm sure they were never lit for the prisoners. Despite a few shafts of natural light coming in from a window way up at the top, it is very dark. I can almost smell the fear and despair that cling to the walls like moisture.

This makes me sad. Standing in the dungeon of Warwick Castle, I realize that so many of us live in private prisons of our own making. Because of disappointments, bad choices, or impossible circumstances, we relegate our hearts to the dark hold below. I look around at the few things that are left in the cold, gloomy cell. They were all once gruesome instruments of torture, used to impose the will of the state on wayward men and women. But, even today, I recognize them, because they still exist in our world. People continue to use them in various forms to torture others. Sometimes, we even use them on ourselves.

TORTURE—THEN AND NOW

As I followed the tour, we came to a set of stone steps in the left corner of the dungeon, leading down to an underground pit. It was just a hole, but I could feel my heart drop down into it. *Oubliette* is a beautiful French word with a terrible definition. It is the word for an ugly, deep, dark hole where you are abandoned—forgotten for good. Sort of like solitary confinement, only worse. It is every woman's greatest fear—abandonment. No one sees, and no one cares. Haven't you been there? You fear that whatever you've done (or whoever you are) is so bad that no one is ever coming for you again. You're totally alone. And somewhere in your mind, you know you deserve it.

Sad to say, the *oubliette* isn't the worst aspect of the dungeon. The next implement of torture I saw was the scolding bridle, a hard metal harness. It was fitted over a prisoner's head, and he or she was led around the city while others shouted insults. Meanwhile the captors called out the crimes the prisoner had committed. In the old days, proof was rarely required for an alleged crime. A woman (or a man) could merely be accused of something and be punished accordingly. Deeds done (and just as many not done) would be announced to all the world, and the accused would be on public display, dragged around in front of everyone in the scolding bridle of shame.

And if shame didn't teach the dungeon dweller a lesson, there was always the hanging chains. This horrific device was a skeleton of metal that covered more than half of the prisoner's body. It hung from the right corner of the dungeon, suspended in midair. An accused criminal would be fitted in these chains and left to hang until death provided release. People sometimes completely broke down just being measured for this brutal device. Once in the chains, the victims hung above the prisoners in the dungeon, forced to look down at the mobility of the others. Their emotions were as tortured as their bodies.

Sound familiar?

In our part of the world, torture is supposed to be illegal. Yet every woman's heart has a dungeon deep inside. Our dungeon can hold us hostage with the shameful wrongs that have been done to us or incarcerate us in an even deeper cell for the sinful things we have done to others or to ourselves. The dungeon can also become a place of self-punishment for a heart that hopes too much. It is the birthplace of cynicism and the breeding ground for despair. The longer we choose to live there, the easier it becomes to push the truths of the fairy tales away—farther and farther out of reach.

THE DENIAL OF RECOGNITION: "YOU'RE NO PRINCESS!"

At breakfast one morning in England, I was writing in my journal. I was in the dining room with a vacationing couple from New York, and we chatted briefly about the usual things. When we had the "what do *you* do?" conversation, I told them I was a writer and that I was there working on a book. They asked politely what I was writing about, and I told them I was developing the idea that every woman is really a princess inside. Before I could say more about the deeper themes of the book, the woman reacted negatively. "In our Jewish-American heritage, that's about the worst thing you can call someone. Being a princess is a bad thing!"

Her husband chimed in and said, "That's right. You're no princess, honey."

We all laughed awkwardly. I'm sure he meant that as a compliment to her, but his words just kept ringing in my head. *"You're no princess, honey."*

I thought how sad it must be for her, and for the rest of us, that the princess has lost her name, and her name has lost its meaning. If her husband had understood what being a princess in your heart really means, he never would have said that to his wife. In essence, he was saying, "I don't see anything different about you, honey. You're really no one special."

It is so much easier to believe that we are not special than to trust that we are. So many negative voices rise up to challenge us if we consider the possibility that "Princess" could be our name. We can find more reasons to believe that we aren't going to be recognized than reasons to trust that we are. When those fears get the best of us, we end up angry or sad that we ever believed we were extraordinary. The truth that we are princesses, recognized by God, is drowned out by the whispers of Warwick.

In our own private dungeon, we slump against the wall and listen.

The *oubliette* whispers, "Forget being recognized; you are forgotten."

The scolding bridle whispers, "Forget being recognized; you have no worth."

The hanging chains whisper, "Forget being recognized; you are left out."

Our deepest disappointments often become our darkest dungeons. The whispers of the *oubliette* and the scolding bridle and the hanging chains don't go away on their own. Left unchecked, the whispers ultimately become louder and more strident. Far from living out a fairy tale, we descend deeper and deeper into the dungeon. Life seems to taunt us because we don't have what we want. We secretly feel worthless and forgotten. Or we see others getting to live their dreams, while we—or so we think—are being punished.

A woman in the dungeon is never grateful. She can't celebrate the good fortune in the lives of others. Instead she allows their fortune to mock her misfortune.

For example, when women struggle with the agony of infertility, it can easily become a dungeon. The pain becomes so great that they can't go to church on

Mother's Day or rejoice over the birth of a friend's child. They're trapped in the dungeon in the hanging chains of envy, and they are not free to celebrate others' joy.

Any woman who longs to be married can end up in the *oubliette*. She thinks every couple is a happy couple and that she has been forgotten. She can't go to dinner with people who are married without feeling despair. The reverse of that situation is also true. A woman in a difficult marriage can feel utterly abandoned. She casts a despairing eye on the single woman. She can't understand why someone who has the chance to go home by herself would have any reason in the world to be unhappy. She, too, feels she's been forgotten.

The woman who is ashamed of her past can be led around in a scolding bridle of shame, allowing the shouts of others to punish her and send her to the dungeon. Real and imagined guilt are woven together into a powerful fabric that is hard to tear through. Sometimes she doesn't even wait for others to harness her; women who have made big mistakes (and most of us have) often lead themselves around in a private world of shame and self-criticism.

A few months ago I came across an article on anorexia. It caught my attention because the writer, who had battled the disease about twenty years ago, wrote, "Anorexia is a last ditch attempt to do something about the badness." She painfully explained that she'd had to confront the way she felt about herself before she could conquer the disease. She said the anorexic "doesn't shed pounds to be beautiful. She sheds pounds as a denial. . . . She does not wish to make herself available for life."

We have to deal with the darkness inside, or it will deal with us. How many women are in the middle of last-ditch attempts to do something about the "badness," locked away in a dungeon, trying desperately to punish themselves enough? Too often it all ends up in a showdown with despair.

What if we could trust that God doesn't punish us like that? Could we stop hurting ourselves? Could we put our trust in his forgiveness and believe that he not only sees us, but he loves us and is taking care of us?

Touring the castle, I came to an upstairs hallway where I saw a huge display case. Probably eight feet long, it housed a unique display of keys. Never have I seen so many keys in one place. Big, fat, hunky keys sitting right next to others that were so delicate and tiny they looked as if they might fit a locket—keys for boxes, rooms, doghouses, everything.

The truths we have discovered in the fairy tales are pure gold. Although we twist them in unrighteousness, they still shine. If the gold is not made into an idol or fashioned into a weapon, it can be forged into a key that will unlock our darkest dungeons.

Remember this, Princess: There's a gold key: You have been recognized. Your crimes *were* enough to put you in the dungeon, but you are not forgotten there. The King has thrown open the door and stepped in to find you. The scolding bridle of shame and guilt has been broken and destroyed. You are loved. Your worth is not determined by your deeds; it is granted by your Father. Your guilt is cleansed by forgiveness. The chains of envy can be melted away by gratitude. Your heart can be *free*, able to grow strong once again.

THE DISMISSAL OF ADORATION:
"THERE IS NO PRINCE!"

I believe that the most lawless and inordinate loves are less contrary to God's will than a self-invited and self-protective lovelessness.
—C. S. LEWIS, *The Four Loves*

Turn on the television, and you can't help but notice that disappointment has never been funnier. It's wonderful to laugh, especially about things we can't change—things that irritate us or make us miserable. There is enormous freedom in chuckling with others, identifying with them over common dilemmas. But much of today's television is tragically funny. We find ourselves laughing when we should be crying. Often it is cheap laughter that comes at the expense of our broken dreams, and we don't even recognize it.

We can't openly laugh at the lack of real intimacy in human relationships; it's too heartbreaking. Besides, it would change any show from a comedy to a drama, so the writers create a funny subworld where no one knows what intimacy really is. That way the characters can tear each other to shreds with verbal insults or have indiscriminate sex, and interestingly enough, no one gets hurt. It's an illusion. Real life tells a different story.

When faced with the idea that one day their prince will come, many women respond with a bitter laugh, laced with cynicism. Our laughter comes at the expense of something very precious to us, whether we know it or not. Most women are jaded about love in direct proportion to their disappointment in men. A friend sent this little mock fairy tale to me.

Once upon a time, in a land far away, a beautiful princess happened upon a frog as she sat contemplating ecological issues on the shores of an unpolluted pond in a verdant meadow near her castle. The frog hopped into the princess's lap and said, "Elegant lady, I was once a handsome prince, until an evil witch cast a spell on me. One kiss from you, however, and I will turn back into the dapper, handsome, and charming young prince that I was, and then, my sweet, we can marry and set up housekeeping in your castle with my mother, where you can prepare my meals, clean my clothes, bear my children, and forever feel grateful and happy doing so."

That night, on a repast of lightly sautéed frog

legs seasoned in a white wine and onion cream sauce, she chuckled to herself and thought, *"I don't think so."*

Laughter is a wonderful balm to soothe pain, but it can also conceal the line that comedy crosses to become tragedy. We'll often laugh with others, then go home and cry ourselves to sleep, mildly aware that we've been had. Our laughter wasn't healing or even a funny distraction. It was despair embezzling our hope. Like enjoying a dinner party only to come home and discover that the person slapping you on the back took all the money out of your wallet. You laughed at the time, but it's not so funny as you realize you don't have your valuables.

If we become so cynical about the idea that any man could ever be a prince, then we resign ourselves to the dungeon of lovelessness. We are no better than the prince in this story, who was looking for a woman to serve him. If we simply expect men to serve us, or we think we exist to remind them that we never will serve them, we are living in the dungeon. We have built a fortress around our hearts. Diametrically opposed to the idealism of making too much of love is the cynicism of not making enough.

Love hurts and disappoints us many times over. That's the truth. That's the awful, painful, heart-breaking truth. But to say that love *always* hurts and disappoints is plain wrong—and self-defeating. Or to imply that because we have not found the love we are looking for, it therefore doesn't exist is equally untrue.

To mock the power of love in the greater human story is to cut off our noses to spite our faces, and forever clip the wings of our hearts.

A friend of mine was telling me about the illness of her friend Joanne. She was explaining Joanne's situation to me and said, *"Of course,* as soon as she got the diagnosis, her husband just up and left her." Part of that statement was the sad truth of Joanne's plight. But it was the "of course" that struck my spirit like an arrow. "Of course" her husband left her? That is not a foregone conclusion. I've known far more men who have stood by their wives in illness than men who have packed a suitcase.

My friend didn't even realize the baseline negativity in her comment. It's not that the husband's action shouldn't be viewed negatively; it's atrocious. But how cynical to interpret his neglect as being the way most men would respond to a wife's illness. Cynicism creeps in and grows around our hearts like poison ivy grows around trees, covering everything said and thought with dark negativity.

"Of course he didn't do what he said he would. He's a *man.*"

"Well, you know Bobby. It's obvious he's cut from the same cloth as his father."

"Yeah, it's too bad their marriage didn't make it. But it figures, doesn't it?"

People don't end up in the dungeon for no reason. Very real wrongs have stolen the most precious things from them. Many disappointments will never be made right. In the awful crimes of sexual or emotional abuse, there is a dark irony that can understandably lead to despair. The offender looks free on the outside while the one hurt ends up in the dungeon, racked by self-hatred and fear. Women who have suffered at the hands of another often keep their hearts locked up their whole lives. Abuse can transport its victim from the innocence of knowing nothing to the cynicism of believing nothing.

But it doesn't have to be that way.

Remember, Princess, another gold key: You are loved. No act of injustice ever done to you has the right to destroy you. Only those things you do in response or the acts you commit against others or yourself can shrink your heart and make it small. Open yourself to love! The golden key of adoration will fit the lock of the most cynical heart. Someday your prince *will* come. He will sweep you up in the wonder of his love. He will not leave if you get sick. He will not make you do all the work while he watches TV. He adores you like no other. Every other love does disappoint us to a certain degree. But this love is different. This is the Prince of heaven, and your heart was made for his love.

THE DEATH OF CONSOLATION:
"ALL WILL *NOT* BE WELL!"

You wake up a little late in the morning because you

accidentally changed Time when you were setting Wake but didn't realize it until you went to make coffee and the microwave clock revealed your error. Never mind that the microwave hasn't worked in a month, the clock keeps perfect time. You start the coffee and know you should stand in the kitchen while it's brewing, because the filter basket is warped from the dishwasher, and it sometimes causes the filter to fold down and let the grounds drop into the pot, but you don't have time. So you get in the shower that doesn't have good pressure (you didn't take a shower during your home inspection before you bought the house) and wonder why you even bother. You realize that you forgot to pick up the cleaning yesterday. Now you have to think about what else to wear, which will probably make you late, and since you've gained ten pounds, will maybe even make you cry. You grab a towel off the rack that has come loose from the wall. You vow to get drywall screws next week but realize that with your mother coming for a visit, you'd better get it done sooner. Sighing, you hurry back to the kitchen to pour your coffee with grinds in it and notice the headline on the front of the paper regarding another horrible shooting at a school. You can't stop the thought from coming as you hang your head with a deep sigh, It's too much. I quit. Nothing is ever going to be right again.

It is hard to believe in happily ever after anymore. And a lot of people don't. They believe it lost the election in the recount or it got destroyed in the document shredder. Just reading the paper is enough to make most people think there is no happy ending to be found. At best it is a myth that makes us feel good. At worst it is a lie that should be exposed.

What Walt Disney did to the fairy tale on one side by making it too perfect, countless film directors have done on the other side by dragging it through the dirt. They make movies and parade them out as the latest version of "reality," when in truth their pictures are propaganda for a world without hope. You are made to feel foolishly naive if you don't subscribe to their unhappy, hopeless conclusions. Not only do the postmodern stories not have happy endings, they don't have happy anything. The portrayals of life in this world are hard, harsh, and empty. If you have been to a movie recently, you may have paid hard-earned money to come out of the theater more confused and troubled than when you went in.

Some of these films are a reaction against the saccharin sweetness of an unrealistic happily ever after, which is understandable and right. But often the stories go way too far to the other side by promoting a world-view of despair and futility. That big red bow that tied everything up neatly is long gone. The bow has been untied and replaced by a strong, tight knot of despair.

Life in the castle oversimplifies, but the underground dungeon intensifies. It makes every issue so complex that there are no suitable answers. Doubt arrives like a storm, and despair settles in behind it like a dark cloud. Doubt and despair are the brother thieves of happily ever after. Doubt isn't necessarily wrong, but when influenced by despair, it can lead a woman directly to the dungeon. She begins to believe that there is nothing and no one guiding the universe, and ultimately life is never going to turn out right.

She sits alone in the dungeon tortured by *Why?* The why questions are just as punishing as thumbscrews or shackles. When we encounter suffering, we often ask, "Why is this happening to me? Why do I deserve this?" We can never fully understand the reasons behind our situation. The castle in the air offers pious explanations, while the dungeon just gives callous responses like, "Sometimes you win, and sometimes you lose."

When I was standing in the dungeon of Warwick Castle, one little girl asked her father, "Daddy, why do people hurt people?"

Her father answered flippantly, "Because they want to."

I wanted to tell him, "That is not an answer; you are going to have to do better than that for your daughter. She deserves more than that. You may not understand it all, but at least try to help her understand what evil is. Please teach her how to recognize it so she can stand up against it. Help her go to sleep tonight with a stronger sense of the power of good and an understanding that you, as her father, will do your best to protect her from evil."

But, I said nothing, and they moved on. I prayed for her question to be answered one day by God himself.

Remember, Princess, a third gold key: All will be well. We have a promise that the King is working things out in the world that we can't see. We will cry now, we will not understand it all, we may think we'll never make it through the storm—but he promises he will never leave us or forsake us. He helps us go to sleep at night with a stronger sense of the power of good and an understanding that he is protecting us from evil. He hasn't assured us that we will always get our way; he has promised that he is the Way. And in his way, despite our suffering, we can safely trust that all will be well.

Many of our dreams will not be completed just yet. But it would make me far sadder to think that there was no hope or dream or prayer that they ever would be completed or fulfilled. We may not get it all in this lifetime. Many of our longings will only be answered and fulfilled in heaven, but that still gives us hope. A day is coming when we will walk free. One day we will be given the desires of our hearts, and our prayers will be answered. So we wait in the hope that God will bring all things to completion, knowing that the greatest and certainly the most lasting completions are yet to come. For only heaven can satisfy and fulfill the deepest desires of our hearts.

If we can acknowledge that what we see in the world is not all there is, we are strengthening our eyes of faith. We can live clinging to the good even when it feels like our fingers are getting rope burn. Whatever we do we can't let go of the truth. In the dungeon, the way out isn't found by lowering our expectations. The way out is through letting the keys open the doors to free our hearts and allowing them to soar upward, toward the goodness they were created to hold.

The woman with a princess heart is no Pollyanna, but she's not the perennial pessimist either. Don't take either fork in the road. Plow straight ahead through the middle, no matter how uncomfortable it gets. Stay down from the castles in the air. Stay above the dungeons in the dark. And don't forget—you have been recognized. You are loved. And one day, all will be well. The golden truths of the fairy tales will clear the path through the middle of the forest and keep you on the right course toward the invisible kingdom, where all princess hearts are called to live.

CHAPTER FIVE

The Invisible Kingdom

I stepped off the plane into another world. Different smells, different cars, different foods all contributed to the realization that this Dorothy wasn't in Kansas anymore. I was in India, a fascinating and unique country, on a trip with a relief organization called World Vision. We had already been several places in the country seeing the organization's work, and now a few of us were taking a side trip to see the Taj Mahal.

For four hours we bumped along a barely paved highway full of camels, cows, other cars, and lots of deep holes. Arriving in Agra, we all felt tired and a little sick from all the bouncing. Part of the tiredness was a soulish sadness from hours of driving through cities of abject poverty. Unfortunately, the scenery in Agra wasn't any better. If anything, because it was a larger city, the conditions were worse—houses with no doors, human waste in the streets, rotten food in the outdoor markets.

Then in the distance, we saw the top of the Taj Mahal rising above the squalor. As we entered through the red-bricked gates, in front of us stood the pristine white, jewel-studded, majestic marble tomb. No picture I'd ever seen had fully captured the beauty in front of my eyes. Yet I couldn't help but feel the savage contrast between this place and the rest of the country. It seemed unreal. Death seemed to be receiving far more glory than life.

It was hard to reconcile the disparity in my spirit. How can you fully enjoy such an opulent wonder when two doors away a mother cannot feed her children? We face similar dilemmas all over the world and even in our own country, but here the contrasts were so sharp. Two distinct worlds—which one is real? The glory and grandeur of death in ages past? Or the present life of poverty and misery? How can they be so far apart? Is there any hope they will ever meet?

Much like the city of Agra and the Taj Mahal, there is a savage contrast between the castles in the air and the dungeons in the dark. They are separate worlds, both holding part of the truth, but neither having it all. In their extremes, each one misses reality.

The castle sets us up to live in an unreal world, while the dungeon drags us down to a world that is too real to survive in. The castle offers the quick fix, the band-aid solutions; the dungeon serves up suffering and the despair of no solutions at all. The castle keeps us hoping in the wrong things, and the dungeon kills our hope altogether. In the castle the make-believe prince looks better than he really is, and in the dungeon, he looks far worse, if there is a prince at all. Good and evil are black and white and easy to spot in the castle, but in the dungeon everything is dingy gray, which ultimately fades to black.

Although there are exceptions to the rule, women tend to gravitate to emotional extremes. We often laugh about this, because we know it to be true. We are either full of hopes and dreams, excited about the future, or we can't get out of bed, believing nothing is ever going to be right again. On good days we poke fun at ourselves, bouncing back and forth. We can start the day in the castle, whistling while we work, and finish the day crying in the dungeon, certain that our lives are over.

Most men, on the other hand, seem to find it easier to maintain a position in the middle. Maybe that's why they don't understand our pull toward the extremes. They have a "one mood all the time" approach to life. Or perhaps they are able to hold more complexity inside without the *need* to figure it all out. If they aren't invited to a certain function, they can still be friends with whoever forgot to include them. How fortunate. This makes men and women entirely different, yet again.

Women can juggle a dinner for ten, watch soccer practice, run a CPA firm, and pick up the dry cleaning by six, but when it comes to emotional issues like love, we narrow it to two extremes. Everything is going to be okay, or nothing matters. We choose the castle or the dungeon. Perhaps for security's sake we are more prone to make a definitive choice than to stand somewhere in the middle.

But stand in the middle we must. As we have seen, there is no life in the extremes. Thankfully, in-between the two lies another world. It is an invisible kingdom that shatters the pretense of the castles in the air and sets us free from the dungeons in the dark. In the invisible kingdom, every woman has a place to stand.

THE PRINCESS OF THE PEOPLE

I got up in the very early hours of July 29, 1981, to turn on my television. Along with 750 million other people, I watched as Diana Spencer married the Prince of Wales. It was a storybook wedding, the likes of which we had never seen. Princess Diana was the first English commoner in three hundred years to marry an heir to the throne. That's what history does for you. On her twenty-five-foot silk taffeta train rode every woman's hopes and dreams.

I was enthralled by the beauty and majesty of it all— the golden carriage, the crimson carpet, the dazzling jewels, and the profusion of flowers. Her veil was held in place by the Spencer family diamond tiara. Holding a bouquet of gardenias, lilies of the valley, white freesia, golden roses, and white orchids, Diana was surrounded by the most beautiful and fragrant flowers in the world.

I wasn't alone in my fascination. I remember my

mother shedding a few tears. I would venture a guess that every woman who saw the royal wedding was deeply touched. As a young girl living in south Louisiana, I was glued to the television to see a world that had only existed in my dreams. Diana was a Cinderella story if there ever was one.

Sadly, as we all know by now, the facts would eventually reveal a dark underside. We would find out that Diana had actually considered calling off the wedding two days before because of Prince Charles's ongoing relationship with Camilla Parker-Bowles. The princess would say later that she considered her wedding day to be one of the most emotionally confusing days of her life.

This was no fairy tale.

She went forward that day with the world watching, and Andrew Morton wrote much later in *Diana*, "The quest of the handsome prince was complete. He had found his fair maiden and the world had its fairy tale. In her ivory tower, Cinderella was unhappy, locked away from her friends, her family and the outside world."

According to most reports, behind the public smiles Diana was a lonely and unhappy young woman. She endured a loveless marriage and was viewed as an outsider by the queen and the rest of the royal family. We eventually saw her desperate need to stop a life of pretense. Even if it embarrassed the royal family, she did not want to live in some castle in the air. Morton wrote, "Daylight has been let in on the magic."

THE PRINCESS OF THE POOR

Another princess was born on August 27, 1910, in what later became Yugoslavia. Her name was Agnes Gonxha Bojaxhiu, but the world would come to know her as Mother Teresa. She also would win the heart of her country, and ours. To the world she would become the face of love to the poor and dying.

In 1950 she sought permission from Rome to start her own order of sisters that would serve those "who, crushed by want and destitution, live in conditions unworthy of human dignity." Thus, the Missionaries of Charity came into existence. They would give love and care to those the world had thrown away. They would willingly enter the dungeons of the crushed and hopeless and set them free.

Two years later she started Nirmal Hriday, a home for the dying in Calcutta. The name literally means "pure heart." It was first located beside a Hindu temple, and the Hindu priests asked the city officials to move the home, creating controversy. Not too long after the decision to leave the home where it was, one of the Hindu priests was discovered to have an advanced stage of tuberculosis. He had been denied a bed in the city hospital because his illness could not be cured. Mother Teresa took care of him herself. When the priest died, she delivered his body to the temple for Hindu rites. "News of this charity filtered out into the city, and Calcutta started its long love affair with the humble sisters."

The following year Mother Teresa opened an orphanage. How opposite of the way the world does things! She chose to care for the dying before turning her concern to the living. Perhaps it was because her mission was to the darkest, deepest corners of despair, which the human soul often encounters in the face of death.

After twenty years of invisibility she was brought into the world's view by Malcolm Muggeridge's 1969 BBC documentary. Two years later, in his book *Something Beautiful for God*, he described how Mother Teresa could "hear in the cry of every abandoned child the cry of the Bethlehem child; recognize in every leper's stumps the hands which once touched sightless eyes and made them see."

In 1979 Mother Teresa won the Nobel Peace Prize. She received the first announcement of the award with these words: "I accept the prize in the name of the poor. The prize is the recognition of the poor world. Jesus said, 'I am hungry, I am naked, I am homeless.' By serving the poor, I am serving Him."

"The saint in a sari" seemed to show up in the strangest places. In 1982 Mother Teresa persuaded Israelis and Palestinians to stop shooting long enough to rescue thirty-seven mentally handicapped children from a hospital in besieged Beirut. In 1985 she was awarded the Medal of Freedom, the highest U.S. civilian award. Her life was a four-foot blue-and-white badge of courage for the world.

Mother Teresa once said, "In these twenty years of work among the people, I have come more and more to realize that it is being unwanted that is the worst disease that any human being can ever experience." Her intention was that all would be received and recognized as people with their own human dignity.

And then the princesses recognized each other. In 1992 the Princess of Wales made a trip to Calcutta. She touched lepers and visited Mother Teresa's hospital for the poor. I can only imagine the connection they felt when they met. Diana, in her princess beauty, was battling the worst disease that Mother Teresa had described—feeling unwanted. And Teresa saw Diana reaching out to touch the poor and standing in the street with lepers, humbling herself to the ground. Heaven was beaming, I'm sure.

One was a princess and the other had a princess heart.

Later, Mother Teresa told Diana during her visit to Rome, "To heal other people you have to suffer yourself." Surely Mother Teresa knew that Diana was suffering. From all accounts she lived in a world where all was not well. Inside the ivory tower she was tired and weary of the charade. A friend said of her life, "She is a prisoner of the system just as surely as any woman incarcerated in Holloway jail."

Mother Teresa saw herself as a pencil in the hand of God. For Diana and countless others, perhaps Mother Teresa's life was more like the handwriting on the wall. She saw poverty as a kind of richness and richness as an impoverishment. "I find the rich much poorer. Sometimes they are more lonely inside. They are never satisfied. They always need something more. I don't say all of them are like that. Everybody is not the same. I find that poverty hard to remove. The hunger for love is much more difficult to remove than the hunger for bread."

By all accounts, the two princesses became friends—the one who denied herself nothing and the one who denied herself everything. Their common ground seemed to be the edges of the invisible kingdom. Diana was looking for it, and Mother Teresa was demonstrating how Diana might open her eyes to find it.

I can only guess that when each stepped into the other's world, everything was turned upside down. Can you picture the leper dying in the street seeing what he must have thought was a vision of Princess Diana? As Her Highness bent low to touch him and offer a soft prayer, his spirit must have soared with the beauty of her grace. And what was it like when Mother Teresa stepped into a formal, royal world of pomp and circumstance dressed in her one-dollar sari? Her very presence called into question the blatant materialism of the modern world. Two princesses in their own right, each revealing different aspects of the invisible kingdom.

Our country got to see them together, not in

celebrity style, but in a poverty-stricken area of the Bronx in June 1997. Once again on their common turf of suffering. Mother Teresa would say later, "She was very much concerned about the poor, that is why she was close to me."

Two months later they would both be gone.

I heard the news of Diana's death on a Sunday morning in a church service. It was almost impossible to believe she had been killed in a car accident. What started as a fairy tale in a carriage ended in a coffin in a castle. She was just thirty-six years old.

Mother Teresa died in Calcutta not many days later, at age eighty-seven, of heart failure. But it was not her heart that failed her. What started in the streets of India ended at the throne of heaven.

For the next week the world mourned the death of two princesses. Each of them had captured the hearts of their countries and the world. Both deaths were covered at length on television, and millions watched the funerals. The spotlight was turned on the contrasts of their lives, which was great, but a few with eyes to see noticed their connection as hunger and healing.

Peggy Noonan wrote, "Saints—like princesses popularly invested with the image of goodness—are even more powerful in death." Born about fifty years apart, living in opposite worlds, they found a connection through the compassion that shaped both of their hearts. One lived in the most visible kingdom in the world, the other in the invisible kingdom. One had beauty and grace on the outside; the other had beauty and grace on the inside. Diana was England's rose, and surely Mother Teresa was India's. The world will never be the same after knowing the Princess of the People and the Princess of the Poor.

OPEN THE EYES OF YOUR HEART

The heart most surely has eyes, for it can see things mere physical sight would never reveal. It is as though a dim and flickering light comes on every once in a while and illuminates things we usually can't see. We easily see a world where the powerful thrive and evil appears to triumph more often than good. But then comes the flicker, and the powerful are brought low, and the poor are exalted—and then it's gone again. It's easy to recognize that image is everything and the beautiful are blessed, and then faintly you see cracks in the image and the hideousness of the so-called beautiful. Once again we are assured that there is another world—one we can't see with our physical eyes.

The dungeon of the real world seems to force our eyes wide open. With twenty-four-hour news coverage on ten different stations, the Internet, radio, and newspapers all bombarding us with images of horrific events, we often see more than we want to. The castles in the air call us to keep our eyes closed tight against all the evil. If we don't see the darkness, it isn't really there. But the invisible kingdom calls us to open the eyes of our hearts, to look at the world honestly, but not to believe that what we can see with our eyes is all there is. We know that one can see without seeing and hear without really hearing. So look underneath and above and all around what you can perceive with your eyes. There is a different world going on, concealed behind the clamor and confusion on the surface.

The apostle Paul wrote that God has invisible attributes, yet they are clearly seen. So they must be in plain sight, yet hidden. Romans 1:20 goes on to say that these attributes can be understood by looking at the things that have been made. When people look at a mountain, some see only a mountain, and others see the majestic handiwork of God. With eyes of faith we can recognize the invisible attributes of Creator God, who fashioned a beautiful world.

When some people walk the streets in India and encounter a beggar, they see only disease and dirt. But when Mother Teresa walked the streets, her eyes saw Jesus in every leper, every orphan, and every outcast. Was she making this up? Or could the eyes of her heart see a deeper reality? For her, reality was the dignity and worth inherent in every human being created in the image of God.

Seeing with the eyes of our hearts reveals the power in unseen things. It reminds us that to understand life we must delve deeper than our circumstances. It allows us to see greater reasons underneath our suffering—reasons that others often miss or ignore. It gives us the chance to see meaning in the events of our lives that we might have overlooked at first glance.

Which is more real, the seen or the unseen? The Thanksgiving food the family shares around the table, or the connection of their hearts amid the feast? Which is the family more hungry for? What about the young mother who changes diapers all day? Does the unseen joy of caring for her precious baby rise above the smell of dirty Huggies? Of course it will if she stays aware of it. But with constant responsibilities and pressures, sometimes we can't keep our vision clear; we become blind. The unseen doesn't clamor for our attention—it never demands that we see it, while what is right in front of our eyes always does.

Jesus spent much of his ministry opening eyes. Maybe he used mud or clay as he was healing, so the blind person could feel the coolness of the mud. Perhaps he wanted them to feel a second layer of blindness so he could demonstrate that he was restoring their physical sight and their spiritual sight at the same time. He wanted all people to see, but more important, he wanted them to see God. He came to restore sight to the spiritually and physically blind and to call into question the proud who said, "I can see just fine, thank you very much." He wanted to train the eyes of their hearts to recognize the invisible kingdom. He knew they wouldn't automatically see those things on their own.

And neither can we. It is through faith that our hearts have the capacity to see the invisible kingdom.

The natural man cannot understand or see the things of the spirit. This is how fairy tales aid us in our faith, by giving us glimpses into another world, stirring up longings for things we can't quite envision.

THE HIDDEN STRENGTH OF HUMILITY

An interviewer once asked Mother Teresa, "Humble as you are, it must be an extraordinary thing to be a vehicle of God's grace in the world."

She replied, "But it is his work. I think God wants to show his greatness by using nothingness."

When Moses asked God for his name, he answered, "I AM WHO I AM." The difference between being a princess and having a princess heart is knowing the difference between the little "I am" and the big "I AM." This creates true humility. The woman with a princess heart is keenly aware that she is great when she is small. She doesn't diminish herself to be so; she simply recognizes that any greatness she has is nothing in light of his greatness. So she is free to be fully herself.

In Lloyd Douglas's book *Magnificent Obsession*, he reveals the strength of humility in the invisible kingdom. Most people, he points out, broadcast their good deeds and hide their bad deeds. What lives on the inside of a person becomes the total of all the things they are hiding. In a sense, you are as sick as your secrets. A heart then is full of the badness tucked away from the rest of the world—even those closest to it.

The greater way to live, he suggests, is to hide your good deeds and openly confess your bad. The strength of a good deed done in secret is increased. When you have done a good deed publicly, you are openly applauded and admired, receiving your credit and any reward right then and there. Then it evaporates. But should you hold good things inside where others do not applaud, the Scripture implies that God applauds. The negative things are confessed, and they evaporate. The good you do in secret then multiplies in your heart and becomes a building block for your character.

Whenever I'm traveling by air, I'm always amazed by the number of people who need to be first to get on the plane. These are people who need to be first at everything. You run into them in the grocery store as they hurry to get into the express line ahead of you. You see them racing toward the elevator to get in before other people. It means so much to them, and I'm not exactly sure why. They act as though someone is going to hand out hundred-dollar bills to the first three people. Of course, getting off a plane, some people have connecting flights and have legitimate reasons to hurry, but I have traveled long enough to recognize them. Other people are not in a hurry; they just believe there is great value in being first or great shame in being last.

There is, in fact, great freedom in *not* having to be first—not in being late or in being left—but in being free, in waiting and trusting. There is freedom when you are not afraid to be wronged, not afraid to be misunderstood, not afraid to be forgotten for the moment. When you can trust that being last doesn't mean you are bad or unloved. When your heart can trust that there is One defender of your reputation when you are maligned, One champion of your heart when you're misunderstood, One kinsman redeemer when you are wronged. That is true liberty and peace. Then you don't have to prove your point, be first off the plane, constantly defend your actions, or demand your rights. You are free to quietly trust.

Jesus taught that those who seek to save their lives will lose them in the grasping. Those who take their place first might be asked to give up their seats later. It may not happen when we can see it, but it will happen. So don't be afraid of coming in last. In the invisible kingdom it means that you will be first in something else. Just smile and enjoy the conversation at the back of the line with some of the greats in the kingdom.

THE BEAUTY OF INVISIBILITY

One woman's story . . . *It happened gradually. I would walk into a room and say something, and no one would notice. I would say, "Turn the TV down, please." And nothing would happen. Then I became more and more aware of it. And not just with the kids. It happened with my husband, too. We had been at a party for about three hours, and I was ready to leave. I looked around and saw he was talking to a friend from work. I walked over, and he kept right on talking. He didn't even turn toward me. That's when I started to put it together:* I'm invisible. I can't believe it. I'm invisible!

Then I saw it everywhere. I walked my son to school, and his teacher said, "Who is that with you, Jake?"

"Oh, nobody."

Nobody. Granted he's five, but it's not just him.

I work to put dinner on the table, and no one acts like anybody put it there. Everybody sits down, and my husband says, "There's no butter." Which means, "I can't see you, and I'm not even addressing you, but when I say there is no butter, the butter lady will get up and get it." Presto, the butter appears, and on we go. No one knows how their socks get back in their drawers, how their favorite treats end up in that mysterious brown bag by the door, who comes to pick them up after school, or why the dog doesn't wet on the rug anymore.

No one sees me. My teenager takes everyone else's advice but mine. My husband talks to other people like he's interested and doesn't even ask me about my day. My preschooler wants to play, but I'm just a body to roll over with the trucks. I am invisible. In a crowded room, no one can see me. I'm just a mother in the grocery store like every other mother, looking for the coupon items. I'm just a wife at a business dinner with every other wife who is bored to death but happy to be out of the house.

I really am invisible . . .

Invisibility is inflicted upon mothers. By the nature of the job, their faces disappear and their work is anonymous. They become hands, building and shaping, fashioning and carving. But what if mothers saw their role like a builder working on one of the great cathedrals? Think about the similarities:

No one can list the names of the people who built the cathedrals. Thousands of people gave their lives to build a monument to God. But there is no record of who they were—no plaques, no certificates, no praise.

They devoted their whole lives to a work they would never see finished. Many of the cathedrals took more than a hundred years to build. A man would start work on this great building knowing he would not live to see what it would ultimately become.

They spent time on details that would never show. When one worker was asked why he was spending time carving the figure of a bird into a piece of wood that would be covered over by the roof and no one would ever see, it is reported that he replied, "Because God sees."

They made great sacrifices for no earthly credit. They had to trust with eyes of faith that what they were doing mattered. They believed the finished work they were helping to create would stand and bring glory to God, which, if you've ever seen them, you know they do.

A WORD TO MOTHERS: TODAY'S BUILDERS

If you close your eyes and listen, you might be able to hear God saying something like this: "I see you; you're not invisible to me. I see the sacrifices you are making. I see your tears of disappointment. You may feel invisible to those around you, but you are never invisible to me. I miss nothing. No act of kindness, no task, no cupcake, no sequin sewn on is too small for me to notice and smile over. You are building a great cathedral. Keep building. You can't see it now, and it will not be finished in your lifetime. You will not have the chance to live there, but if you build it well, I will."

Invisibility is not an affliction. It is not a disease that erases your life. It is the cure for the real disease of self-centeredness. It is the antidote to pride. It is an invitation to let humility be made flesh. We are never more beautifully invisible than when we are on our knees. People around us don't have to see us; they can't. But we don't work for them anyway; we work for him, and he sees everything.

Let me be invisible, Lord. Let me love the things that no one sees. Let me be more invisible in you that I may love others more visibly. Let my work stand as a great monument to an even greater God.

MORE TO LIFE THAN MEETS THE EYE

A woman with a princess heart sees the world through the eyes of faith. She is a citizen in the invisible kingdom. She sees the hard realities of the world with her eyes open, yet looks deeper to take note of the beauty and grace hidden underneath.

Any woman seeking to be a princess will live alone

in the visible kingdom, surrounded by "stuff" that others can see. But a woman cultivating a princess heart will live invisibly, trusting that there is more to life than what can be seen. An insecure princess will flaunt her good deeds, but the woman with a princess heart will hold them close to herself. A spoiled princess might demand to be first, but the one with a princess heart is free to be last, confident that she is loved.

Life is never going to be perfect in the here and now, but that is no reason to give up. Somewhere between our young idealism and our midlife cynicism is *life*. Right now we see life through a dark glass. We have some light, but we can't see it all. What we can see is that the world we live in contradicts the way life should be, and it creates the yearning for what it will be one day. Life is full of faint memories of what we've lost and faint signals that point forward to what still lies ahead.

For now we know in part. We can't hold on to the past, nor can we predict the future. We aren't what we were, but we are not what we will be either. We don't have to pretend, and we don't have to give up. We can stand in-between the "no longer" and the "not yet." We must stand courageously in the present, looking backward and forward at the same time.

The woman with a princess heart *remembers*. She doesn't try to live in the past, in a world that no longer exists, but she never forgets the past. She remembers the past often, giving thanks to the King for how far he has brought her in the journey.

She *longs* for what is to come. She yearns for the day when all will be well. She awaits a time when the desires of her heart will be filled and all her longings will come into their own. She aches over the unfulfilled places but never despises the hoping.

The one with the princess heart *waits*. She lives in-between remembering the past and hoping for the future. She is not fully satisfied in the here and now, but she is content to wait for what is to come. She recognizes that she knows only "in part," so she lives trusting in the promises of the King.

CITIZENS OF TWO WORLDS

As I left India, that country of savage contrasts, I thought again of Mother Teresa. She had a dual citizenship—her body living and working in the slums of India while her heart lived in the invisible kingdom. Through her life's work, she built a great monument to God. It has not gone unnoticed. The chairman of the Nobel committee said, "Mother Teresa has personally succeeded in bridging the gulf that exists between the rich nations and the poor nations. Her view of the dignity of man has built a bridge."

We, too, are called to dual citizenship. We, too, are called to build a bridge. Oh that we might have the eyes of faith to see the invisible kingdom that lives between our city of Agra and our Taj Mahal. That we might see Jesus in the eyes of a dying man who bears no physical resemblance to the Savior, or recognize the hunger for love in the eyes of a princess who seems to have everything. That we might hold a view of human dignity given us by God.

The same God who inspired the great cathedrals is the One who knelt down to touch and heal the wounds of the lepers. In him, Mother Teresa found her place to stand in the tension between the two worlds. In him, we can find ours. Mother Teresa illuminated the way down from the castles in the air and shone a light on the way up from the dungeons in the dark, finding a way to the solid ground of the invisible kingdom on earth. She has given us a beautiful example of a true princess heart thriving in a not-so-fairy-tale world.

CHAPTER SIX

You Are A Princess

She is standing on the tarmac of the LAX runway with a baton in her hand helping to bring my plane to the gate. I'm watching her, and she's watching the wheels and the wing of the aircraft while motioning it forward with the stick. It seems like an invisible job to me, and I wonder if she minds it. She has beautiful, long, dark hair, and I wonder if she ever doubts her beauty. I wonder if she hears compliments from her friends. I wonder if she laughs freely and loudly or if she's quiet around her family. I wonder if she goes home after work to someone who adores and appreciates her. I wonder if she works with people who think she is special. I wonder if she knows God has named her a princess. I silently pray that if she doesn't, she soon will.

I was first drawn to the writings of George MacDonald by the titles of his books. Every time I read a list of his works, I saw another book about a princess. I knew a little about George MacDonald from coming across his name in others' books—that he was an eighteenth-century poet and preacher. And I'd read excerpts from some of his books and sermons. But the first fiction work I read of MacDonald's was a little fairy tale called *The Lost Princess*.

Years later when I started working on this book, I discovered that he was consistently praised by C. S. Lewis and G. K. Chesterton for his fairy tales. Surprisingly, at least ten of his fairy tales have "princess" in the title. How interesting that a Scottish minister would devote so much of his writing to princesses. It made perfect sense when I came across something Chesterton wrote about MacDonald's stories:

> The commonplace allegory takes what it regards as the commonplaces or conventions necessary to ordinary men and women, and tries to make them pleasant or picturesque by dressing them up as princesses or goblins or good fairies. But George MacDonald did really believe that people were princesses and goblins and good fairies, and he dressed them up as ordinary men and women. The fairy tale was the inside of the ordinary story and not the outside.

Can you see the mark of the invisible kingdom? The world sees ordinary people going about their days and tasks and recognizes a few extraordinary ones when they dress up on the outside in remarkable clothes or noteworthy accomplishments.

George MacDonald saw the world quite differently. He saw every woman as a beautiful princess dressing down on the outside as an ordinary mother or lawyer or teacher. He believed that in the invisible kingdom, the greater strength of people came from what was in their hearts, as opposed to anything that was in their wallets or in their closets or on their résumés. Do we dare believe such good news today? That every woman is a princess walking in this world with that kind of identity? What could that mean to a woman's heart? How would belief in that truth change her thoughts, not to mention her spirit and her relationships?

THE PRINCESS CONFUSION

The very word *princess* is in danger of going the way of other beautiful and meaningful symbols trying to survive in a world of image. Our symbols—*princess* is only one example—have a tendency either to become remote and unattainable, except for the privileged few, or they become so common that they are cheap and tawdry. It is the tug of war in our culture to push things high and out of reach or pull them down to the mud.

In the South, where I grew up, our princesses were Southern belles. The very idea of a common girl being thought of as a princess was absurd. The qualifications were clear. Your name mattered (and not just your last name, but all twenty of your names, dating back to the Civil War). Your manners mattered (not as much as your name but a close second), and your money mattered (not as much as your manners, because there were enough people making the rules who didn't have money).

In her wonderful, wry, if not sad, book *A Southern Belle Primer*, Maryln Schwartz explains these impossible rules. The royal House of Windsor has nothing on the princesses of the South, as evidenced by her subtitle, *Or Why Princess Margaret Will Never Be a Kappa Kappa Gamma*. She tells how Her Royal Highness Princess Margaret walked around the living room of the president of the Neiman Marcus stores with a lighted cigarette. "That woman may be the sister of the Queen of England. She may be the relative of the last czar of Russia. She may even have a closet full of diamond tiaras. But the Southern belles in that room knew without a doubt—that woman would never make a sorority at the University of Texas."

In the South so many things can disqualify you from being a princess—even if you really are one, as Princess Margaret was. Select the wrong silver pattern, put dark meat in your chicken salad, wear white shoes after Labor Day, or use Miracle Whip for anything, and you are out of the running.

But if our world isn't putting the idea of princess out of reach, then it seems to be bringing it low and tarnishing the image beyond repair. It probably wasn't a good idea for me to do an Internet search on the word *princess*. I can't begin to tell you all the things that name pulls up—many of them not so savory. And very few Web sites would help us understand what the real identity of a princess is or what her heart is about. Unfortunately, most of them could be filed under "how the princess has come down in the world." I was too cautious to enter "Snow White" in a search, for fear of what it would bring up.

Besides the more degrading ones, many of the princess links were pathetic attempts to identify with something noble. Princess, the dog, was rescued by the humane society and now has her own Web page. Princess Cruise Lines promises to treat you like royalty. You can even pick your own Hollywood princess. This is a site where you take on an Internet identity of some misguided L. A. starlet, who has less in common with a princess than the little dog from the humane society.

I even found the official Web site of the Jewish American princesses. It is a very funny site, which includes their complete recipe book of what to make for dinner every night—reservations. It also includes a few funny ways to tell if you are a Jewish American princess . . .

If you've had diamond studs soldered into your earlobes . . .

If your dog owns more clothing and toys than your neighbor's children . . .

Of course we've all seen tee-shirts and bathrobes,

halter tops and thongs emblazoned with the word *princess,* sometimes even in rhinestones. But its use on these items is just a word, not a name. What it means is so cheapened by its commonness that it has nothing to offer us. Far from elevating the idea of the princess, the culture tattoos it everywhere but on the one place it matters the most: our hearts.

Many of our deepest symbols and values are struggling to survive in this cultural tug of war. It is a sad fact of our world that what we can't attain we level. We pull noble things to the ground so they won't intimidate us. And once we have them on the ground, we trample them or reduce them to a bumper sticker or burn them on television or just casually walk back and forth over them until the higher meaning is gone and the symbol lies deflated and battered in the dirt. Then we wonder why there is so little meaning in anything.

When symbols are separated from their deeper meaning, either by being placed out of reach or cheapened to irrelevance, then only the image of the thing is left. We are living in a culture where image is everything. Because of this, the idea of having a princess heart is far less attractive than putting on a princess *face.*

ALL THAT GLITTERS

The face of where we live has changed the face we live with. Life used to be lived in small towns in the country, and now it's moved to the large cities and their suburbs. People live in twenty different places over their lifetime and sometimes work almost as many different jobs. We've literally left face-to-face relationships that were stable and consistent to make fast, superficial, largely anonymous acquaintances. What used to be called character has crumbled at the feet of personality and image. A first impression is all there ever will be, so you must put your best face forward. And plastic surgeons all over the country will help you do that. But are we dragging down our hearts as we lift up everything else?

Erma Bombeck was catapulted to success by her witty and honest writing about aging and its difficulties. She made us laugh out loud as she gave words to help us see that the wrinkles on our faces, the bumps in our noses, small lips, sagging breasts, and the general spreading out of everything were realities of this earthly life to be borne with dignity and humor. We can laugh about the things we can't change. Or can we?

No longer, it would seem. It's difficult to make jokes about any of these things anymore because they are changeable. You can get your nose done, your breasts enlarged, and your tummy tucked. So where is the humor in our aging these days? If these things are changeable, then we are held responsible and even thought foolish if we don't do something about them.

Cosmetic surgery started as the humane treatment of wartime injuries. Today it is a multibillion-dollar industry that is practiced mostly on those in good health. The number of people going in for surgery has tripled in the last ten years. And, surprisingly, the largest percentage of those going in for the most popular procedures—nose jobs and breast enlargements—are between the ages of nineteen and thirty-four.

The word *cosmetic* is defined as something used or done to cover up defects. And this raises some interesting questions: Are wrinkles defects? Are small breasts a fault? Has age become a flaw? We used to think of flaws in terms of a person's character, not a person's appearance. Nowadays no one seems sure which is more egregious, immorality or crow's feet.

I went to the dermatologist to have a mole removed and noticed a brochure for BOTOX. It had a picture of a woman my age with the furrowed crease in her brow that most of us have from college on. She looked just like me when I worry about getting older. The ad read, "It takes thirty-five years to get it, and ten minutes to get rid of it." The ad was subtly asking every woman, why wouldn't you do something about this wrinkle? Never mind that it means having botulism injected into your muscle. Never mind the danger of numbness and loss of feeling in your forehead. Go ahead and spend your money on what your forehead looks like from the front, instead of taking better care of what is behind it.

Surveys show that women are overwhelmingly more favorable toward cosmetic surgery today than they were ten years ago and that the main obstacle for most women is the cost. What is wrong with us? Have we completely given up on the value of what is inside of us, trading it for what can be seen on the outside? A woman can go to a surgeon to make herself beautiful, but a surgeon is powerless to cause even the ugliest man to love her.

Our preoccupation with appearance indicates how terrified we are of being forgotten or becoming invisible or merely going unnoticed. If this weren't the case, why would so many try to hide it? Around Hollywood, it's commonly said that it's easier to count the people who have never gone near the knife than those for whom it's a ritual. But it is no secret that all over town, discreet little hotels advertise their availability for plastic surgery recovery—back entrances, registration under false names, round-the-clock nursing with no questions asked.

Plastic surgery is no longer medicine; it has become a fashion accessory. And it is sometimes a disgusting one at that, as collagen-inflated lips turn a normal smile into a grotesque mask. But that's not the end of it. A recent magazine article reports, "Since collagen has only a short-term effect, surgeons have already gone on to more drastic remedies: Fat suctioned from other parts of the body—the thighs or the rear—ends up being injected into the mouth."

And it gets even crazier. "There's a substance called alloderm, which is actually strips of skin recycled from cadavers. Plastic surgeons tunnel it in strips through the lips, starting at the corners of the mouth. It results in the same puffed-up pouter, but this stuff stays around longer."

Upturn the nose, please. Implant new cheekbones. Would you like the princess face of Audrey Hepburn? Welcome to the cathedral of image. We hope you'll worship with us. Our high priest is a plastic surgeon, and our salvation is perfection. We are a proud community of purchased beauty. We have our own patron saints like Hollywood stars and celebrities who point the way to redemption. We believe you are only as old as you look. Clergy will meet with you privately to advise how to take away your infirmities. After all we are fallen in two ways, but we certainly don't have to look it in one. And about that tummy? Why suck it in when you can tuck it in instead? Don't worry about all the feeling you are losing; you won't need it in the long run.

Society's prizing of eternal youth makes aging our enemy, and that is unfortunate. We are at war with the natural process of our own bodies. Everything about this world is fallen, and we all have the sags to prove it. Have you ever noticed that *gravity* rhymes with *depravity?* Our bodies suffer as well as our souls under the weight of a world that should have been otherwise. But surgery is not the answer. It is a high-dollar denial that disconnects our inside from our outside. There is no salvation under the knife because the tissue is not the issue. The deeper issue lies in our hearts.

THE PRINCESS HEART

As [a woman] thinketh in [her] heart, so is [she].
—PROVERBS 23:7 (KJV)

Snow White was the fairy tale that started it all. In 1937, Walt Disney produced the first animated motion picture, but the story was published by the Grimm brothers in 1812 and illuminated perfectly the age-old conflict between image and heart. Snow White was a beautiful little princess who grew up happily despite living with an awful stepmother. This cruel woman was a vain queen and dressed Snow White in rags to hide and undermine the little girl's beauty, which the story says came from her goodness. The queen was enthralled with her own appearance and obsessed with maintaining her beauty.

Every day she would ask, "Mirror, mirror on the wall, who's the fairest one of all?"

And every day the magic mirror would reply, "You are the fairest one of all."

Then one day the mirror answered differently. It informed her, "Snow White is the fairest in the land." The queen was wild with jealousy and began to plot how to get rid of Snow White. She sent her huntsman to take Snow White into the woods and kill her, ordering him to bring back the little girl's heart as proof that she was dead.

Snow White's heart was what threatened the queen

the most. The girl was beautiful, but it was her heart that made her so. The queen wanted to possess the heart of Snow White, because it was the heart of a princess.

Some women have criticized fairy tales for their portrayal of women. They have pointed out that all the old women in fairy tales are ugly and mean and cruel while the good characters are all young and beautiful and innocent. But they misunderstand the fairy-tale world. Isn't it the condition of our hearts that determines which character we identify with?

The queen isn't wicked because she's old; she's wicked because she's vain and heartless and that kills the youthful spirit in her. Unfortunately, wickedness of any kind will harden with age—but wickedness is the problem, not age. An older woman with a princess heart can watch a Snow White at any age, without envy, and still see herself as the one with dreams and hopes. But when our hopes have died and we've covered hardened hearts with beguiling images and constant comparisons, it's far harder to identify with Snow White, and far easier to envy those who are still young and innocent and dreaming.

As we think in our hearts, so are we.

A TRUE REFLECTION

Goethe wrote that what a person sees in others reveals what is in his own heart. He was echoing what we read in Proverbs 27:19, which says,

As in water face reflects face,
So the heart of man reflects man.

A face sometimes reflects only a face, especially in this age of image, but what ultimately reveals the person is the heart. If the heart is dark, it sees only darkness and makes the face dark too. Through cosmetics, the defect can be corrected, right? No, because the real defect is never on the outside but on the inside. Change our hearts, and our faces change too. In fact, the way we view life and God changes entirely. What is in our hearts reflects how we view God. As Oswald Chambers wrote, "God's revelation of Himself to me is determined by my character, not by God's character. 'Tis because I am mean, Thy ways so oft look mean to me."

We don't need more cosmetics on the outside. We don't need more social rules to keep. We need what can only happen in our hearts when God speaks to us. At the sound of his voice, image crumbles at the feet of true substance. Hurt is happily traded for hope. The heart finally finds its worth. And the princess finally learns her name.

WHAT'S IN A NAME?

Why is it important to be called or named a princess? Just think for a moment about what names mean to us. Almost everything has a name, and if it doesn't, we give it one. We name our children, our pets, and our stuff. People name things they love in order to claim them and care for them. Our children name their dolls and toys. A name gives dignity and value.

I have a dear friend who calls me Nikki. No one else has ever called me Nikki, and that's why she calls me that name. It's her name for me. In England, homes are given names like Bramble Cottage or Ennis Keep. Francis of Assisi used to name everything when he spoke to it, making it personal by saying, for example, "Brother Sun" or "Sister Bird." Some people refer to their automobiles by name, saying something like, "Where should we park Major?" They treat an inanimate object like a friend because of their affection for it.

This is especially refreshing in our society, where many people treat friends like inanimate objects. Numbers have replaced names, and people *assign* value rather than recognize value. That is backward. You have a Social Security number, a phone number, a customer number, an order number, but you are a person, not a number, for you have a name. A number is never a name, nor can it adequately represent your name. Numbers are dehumanizing. Statistics don't breathe or feel. They have no inherent dignity or value, only what is assigned them. Names are personal and meaningful.

It's hard to recognize the value of a name in our present culture, because *what you do* seems more important than *who you are*. But what you do is not who you are; it's only a label. Beautician, agent, lawyer, mother—none of these is your name.

A parent names a child with hope and promise. Children learn their names and grow into them—they become their names. A child practices writing her name as soon as she is able. The name is not the symbol of the person; it *is* the person. Ultimately she signs life's most important documents with her name. It is her word, it is her identity, it is who she is. And as life goes on, we can't imagine her being called anything else.

I asked my mother how she chose the name Nicole for me. She smiled and said she read it in a book and thought it was beautiful. My middle name, Ashley, came from a name listed inside our family Bible, and she thought the two names went well together. She couldn't have known what a 'Nicole Ashley' would be like or what I would do for a living, but in faith, with hearts of love, it's who my parents wanted me to be. At this point in my life I can't imagine having any other name. It's me.

A name asserts that a new life is beginning, a new identity is coming into being. When God called Abram to himself, he gave him a new name, Abraham, and promised him that he would be the father of many nations. When parents bring a new life into the world, they give their child a name. When priests or nuns take their monastic vows, they choose a new name to signify a new life.

We are namers, because God was a namer. He brought Adam into existence and gave him his name. Then God allowed Adam to name the animals for him. "And whatever the man called each living creature, that was its name." (Genesis 2:19 NIV) And then just one chapter later after the Fall, Adam is hiding among the trees in the Garden of Eden. The Lord calls directly to Adam. He says, "Where are you?" God didn't say, "Human being that I have created, come out of the bushes!" He spoke to him personally. He had created him and knew him as Adam. He spoke to him as Adam. God has done this since the beginning of time. The unique value and dignity of human life came from our Creator. While the Bible is full of all those genealogies that we like to skip over, they demonstrate the importance of our names in the eyes of God.

NAMED BY GOD

In Isaiah 45:4, God says to Cyrus, "I have even called you by your name; I have named you, though you have not known Me" (NKJV).

Regardless of whether we know him, he knows us.

The place we're in right now is unique. On one hand we are not where we once were, thank goodness. We can all look back and see things we've done wrong and things we wish we'd done differently. But these things can be forgiven so that we have no regrets. On the other hand, we are not where we will be either. Only God can see what the future holds for each of us. So he waits for a moment like this one when he has our heart's attention, and then he tells us some things.

God tells us that he knew us in our mother's womb.

That he smiled at our birth and that he knows everything about us. That he sees our aspirations and our
dreams, our struggles to keep our hearts from pretending or denying. He tells us that he knows us, even
better than we know ourselves. And best of all, he
knows something beyond what we know: He knows
what he is calling us to become.

At this crossroads, then, God whispers something
in our ears that can change our hearts forever. The
Lord of the universe, the Creator of heaven and earth
draws near to our hoping, trembling hearts and
whispers one word: *princess.*

Heaven holds its breath as he speaks a name that is
deeper than our gifts or abilities; a name that gives us
our place and purpose in the world. For a woman, it is a
portrait of her heart and soul, which belongs only to her
and to no one else in the same way. It expresses the
nature, the character, and the life purpose of the woman
who bears it. To paraphrase George MacDonald, "Who
can give a woman this, her own name? God alone. For
no one but God knows and delights in who she is, and
who she will become."

No one but God can recognize you fully.

No one but God can love you so completely.

No one but God can fulfill your heart's deepest
desires.

No one but God can name you Princess.

Despite today's distortions, the princess has been
the most adored figure throughout most of history.

Royal, beautiful, and admired, she holds the hopes and dreams of her country in her heart and in her smile. Not yet a queen, her life is rich with possibility and promise and, one day, a throne. Daughter of the King, loved by the people, sought by every prince in the land. With beauty and poise and strength, she bestows honor and grace. She is confident and radiant and courageous.

Of course, in the upside-down way of the invisible kingdom, we do not make a name for ourselves. That would be silly. Instead, we discover the King's name for us. Through a staggering miracle, God calls us his beloved daughters, making each of us a princess in our own right. When he names us, we begin the adventure of being who we are and becoming who we will be. A princess discovers her princess heart as she grows into her name.

BELIEVING YOUR NAME

God calls us Princess because that is who we are before him. It's not a make-believe, flattering word meant to buoy our spirits so we don't wake up depressed every day. But, naturally, it lifts our spirits and changes our perspective and helps us rise above doubt and depression. To be named by God means to know who we are and to be free to be who we are. Free from the past to start over. Free to become what he has in mind for us.

Princess is not a name in some social "blue book"

that puts you in a prominent family. You are placed by grace in the middle of the royal family of God with everyone else who doesn't deserve to be there. You didn't get invited because of your chicken salad, and you don't stay in the family because you dress like Diana. Our name, our worth, and our true identity are never based on anything external. Our name is not an achievement like being inducted into a hall of fame. It's a gift. And we cannot pay anything in return, except in gratitude to become who we are. We honor the name we have been given by living it out. We can never become a princess by putting on airs or the pretentious manners of a princess but rather by discovering ourselves and blossoming into the princess the King has called us to be.

I am writing this book by faith. I'm not sure what it looks like to live every day believing our name, believing who God says we are, because there are days when I have my doubts. There is no formula to follow, because becoming our name looks different for each of us. But I do know that as we trust our name, instead of doubting it, everything can change. When I trust that I am chosen, graced, and beloved of God, I feel more myself than when I am full of doubt and insecurity. So I side with God and his name for me rather than with my fear.

So what if I believe that God has named me and given me a princess heart, and then I find out I'm just ordinary me? Who cares? But if I live every day as ordinary me, doubting my worth and my ability to affect the world for good, and I miss the chance to really live—for that I would feel a sorrow deeper than words can describe. So I choose a life of faith and stake my heart, like a young oak tree, on the claims I believe to be true. Then I can spend my greatest energy not on proving these claims, but on growing up, supported by their strength, to become exactly the woman that he made me to be.

THE INVISIBLE PRINCESS

Let me know you, for you are the God who knows me; let me recognize you as you have recognized me. You are the power of my soul; come into it and make it fit for yourself, so that you may have it and hold it without stain or wrinkle.
—AUGUSTINE, *Confessions*

With a princess heart we no longer have to live with any concern for our own image or reputation. We live for the approval of the One who named us, the One who recognized us. It is his recognition that matters, not our own. It is his renown that we are after. Our own accomplishments need not be trumpeted anymore—they don't create our worth; that is settled by our name. We don't have to fret over our faces, because they are a reflection of our hearts, not the definition of our value. We are free, gloriously free to be ourselves as he sees us. We can, as Proverbs 27:2 advises, let others' lips praise us and not our own.

The princess heart is our invisible nature as a member of the royal family. It is never a badge or a label to slap on in public. It is a secret name that acts like a passport to an alternative world, in-between the castles in the air and the dungeon. If we try to alter that and flaunt the name Princess as a public statement, it loses its power. It's not a tee-shirt or a bumper sticker or a set of assumed manners. If it becomes any of those things, it ceases to be God's name for us and becomes a pose we assume for ourselves. Only trouble lies down that path.

So we live each day trusting our identity and membership in the invisible kingdom. We see with the eyes of our hearts all the unseen things that others miss. We descend to greatness through humility and bask in the freedom not to have to be best and be first. And we know that the more we live content with our invisible selves, the more beautiful we are to God.

In *The Spirit of the Disciplines,* Dallas Willard writes, "Secrecy rightly practiced enables us to place our public relations department entirely in the hands of God, who lit our candles so we could be the light of the world, not so we could hide under a bushel. We allow him to decide when our deeds will be known and when our light will be noticed." And we know from our own special fairy tale that our light will be noticed in due time. And when God makes it shine, it really shines, and no one can miss it.

When he goes into the woods, the huntsman who has been ordered by the queen to kill Snow White cannot do it. He recognizes her princess heart. He breaks down sobbing because he cannot commit such an evil act, and he sets her free. He returns to the queen with a heart, but it is the heart of a doe instead. Sounds a lot like God's provision for each of us. The wicked queen's murderous plan was thwarted, and evil did not prevail over the princess heart.

I'll admit, when it comes to recognizing princesses, Disney has a pretty good public relations department. Watching the movie recently, I noticed one other tiny detail that I had missed all those years watching *Snow White*. The seven dwarfs go to work every day in a mine—a diamond mine. They recognized value when they saw it in Snow White! No one told them she was a princess, and she never mentioned it, but they could see her heart shine as brilliantly as the diamonds they mined every day.

As for us, when it comes to recognizing princess hearts, God has a better PR department than Walt Disney could ever imagine.

GUARD YOUR PRINCESS HEART

A princess heart needs to be guarded, not just grown. A princess is not a commoner, and common things, common relationships, or common deeds are not for her. She must guard her heart against whatever is not worthy, against whatever is not royal or noble, against anything that would discredit the King.

She will do well to keep her heart in the invisible kingdom where it never wrinkles or sags or stretches. Always out from under the knife of image, she can consistently strengthen it with good deeds done in secret. Her heart will befriend her face and her body, realizing they are not her enemies. Neither is age an enemy, nor wrinkles. She will call off the war and set up peace talks between the inside and the outside. She knows that both can beautifully reflect the One who made her.

The outward circumstances, even the appearance of a princess, will change based on things that are beyond our control. But the princess heart, when it is guarded, only grows and blossoms. So we put confidence in our name and even more confidence in the One who named us. It is the greatest gift of our lives, providing sure footing in this slippery world. He named us before we were born, and only he sees who we will become. And at every opportunity given to him, he whispers it again and again to our hearts. "Princess . . . You are a princess."

From my window seat I glance once more at the tarmac at LAX. The princess is still standing there disguised, dressed down in her ordinary work uniform. And despite the commercial earplugs she is wearing, I hope that today will be the day she hears the King whisper her name.

CHAPTER SEVEN

Someday My Prince Will Come

Standing in the kitchen in a tattered bathrobe, she rinsed out her coffee cup. The kids were on the bus with their lunches, her husband was stuck in commuter traffic, and the dog was looking up at her, waiting for his food. If you had asked her, she wouldn't have even known she was humming as she opened the dog-food can. But a smile might have played across her lips if you had told her she was humming "Someday My Prince Will Come" . . .

Larry Morey and Frank Churchill had no idea what they were putting into words when they penned the famous song for the 1937 film *Snow White and the Seven Dwarfs*. How could they have known what those words would stir up? Their song put a voice to a desire greater than either the words or the music.

Every good fairy tale has a prince—Prince Charming, Prince Wesley, Prince Caspian. Many have no name at all—they are simply referred to as "the prince." But in almost every story, no matter his name, he goes about doing two things: finding and rescuing. These are the tasks and the joys of a prince. He will find the princess and rescue her from her situation: lovelessness, boredom, poison apples, or sleeping disorders, to name only a few.

Women are responders. Now please don't get me wrong. We are strong, capable initiators, and we can hold our own in almost every situation. We are determined, forceful, and talented. But when it comes to love, we want to respond. We want to be found and, yes, in more ways than we'd like to admit, *rescued* by a prince. We don't want to sweep; we want to be swept away. We don't want to catch as much as we want to be caught up. We like to draw, but not as much as we like to be drawn in. We may search, but our hearts long to be searched for. We want to be looked after, talked to, turned on, thought about, and prayed over—all of which amount to responding rather than initiating. We may be modern women, but our hearts are still full of timeless desires.

We want more than *just* that, which is where some of our problems come in, but there is no greater thrill than being discovered by a prince. A woman can't help but respond to a heart that has come looking for her heart. As she loves in return, nothing compares to the wild satisfaction she feels in responding. But it must be true response and not something she has sought or pursued or manipulated.

Women don't want to ask to be found, just as men don't want to admit to being lost. Having to ask says something about us that we don't like. When a man has to ask for directions, he is forced to face his limitations. Asking broadcasts to the world that he doesn't know where he is. He is a finder, and what finder wants to admit he can't find himself?

In the same way, when a woman has to ask her love to find *her*, it takes away every ounce of thrill from being found. For both of them, the asking is the problem, which leads to arguments like, "If I have to ask, it just isn't worth it." And many times it isn't. Asking takes the joy out of being fully man or fully woman. The man is not free to find where he is going, which is part of his nature. And the woman is not free to be found, which is part of hers.

We love what being found brings out in us. When a woman knows she is loved, she is set free to be her fullest human self. She becomes generous and kind in ways she may not have been before. Her spirit is lifted, her step is quicker, and her heart is glad. To feel cared for and known, loved and embraced, cherished and valued—*to be found*—releases her. It softens her, tames her critical spirit, and sets her free to soar on the wings of life. Undisputedly the supreme human emotion, love holds the rousing possibility of unleashing rivers of joy.

But love can also carve deep canyons of sorrow in our souls. A woman cannot make anyone come looking for her. And without the heart of another to pour love out on her, she cannot feel loved. Love takes two: one to find, and one to be found.

Because love is about receiving and giving, even if we have not been found, we can still give love away. True, it is harder—it's far easier to give out of the abundance of what we have been given. But it is not impossible. We can freely love others. We can love the poor. We can love our enemies. And we certainly can love ourselves. We do not have to wait to be loved in order to give love away.

But when it comes to receiving, we are stuck. We can't create a heart that searches for us. That heart must find us first. That heart must discover our heart. That love must be looking for our love. And when the heart full of love recognizes the heart wanting to be loved, the only appropriate response is to respond. This is how we are created.

But we must always remember that we live in a world that should have been otherwise. Too often we don't want to wait to be found. We don't want to wait to be rescued or admit that we need to be. That makes us too vulnerable and too dependent. The modern world and our hearts' real desires are often set at odds—like the first toaster I had. It wasn't made for bagels. Trying to get the bagel and the toaster to cooperate was not only damaging to both, it was a fire hazard. And with love, the pain of waiting for a prince to find you can overshadow the hope of his arriving. This can make a woman so angry that if a prince actually does arrive, she may well scare him off before he can rescue anything.

This turns up the volume on our difficulty. How can we respond when there is nothing to respond to? How can we be found when it seems no one is looking for us? How long can our hearts wait when they're not sure who or what they're waiting for?

BACK TO THE GLASS SLIPPER

There was a man who took for his second wife a haughty woman. He had a young daughter, who was gentle and sweet natured. She took after her mother, who had been the best person in the world. After the father died, the little girl didn't fit in the new family and was made to do all the work because the stepmother favored her own two daughters.

When the girl was finally finished with all her work, she would retire to the chimney corner and sit in the cinders. Because she was dirty and smelled like smoke, they called her Cinderella. The poor girl lived a miserable existence. But with each new dawn, somehow Cinderella found new hope, and she worked away, unrecognized and invisible. No matter what sort of insults or pranks her stepfamily pulled, no matter how hard they made her work, she remained sweet and kind.

Then came the day that the king announced there would be a ball at the castle. The sisters fussed over what they were going to wear. They teased Cinderella mercilessly about what she planned to wear to the ball, knowing very well that she wasn't going. Who could imagine someone like her attending the king's ball?

Everyone headed out for the festivities, and Cinderella was left crying in the garden. The stepmother and the sisters had put every obstacle in her way, and she was sitting alone sobbing. The fairy godmother saw her. Really saw her. With a little magic, she helped the outside match the inside. The young girl was transformed. She was dressed in a glorious gown that matched the riches of her heart, and she was on her way to the ball. For the first time in her life Cinderella had been lifted from the ashes.

Inside at the ball, the prince was informed that a grand princess had arrived whom no one knew, and he went out to welcome her. He recognized immediately that she was not ordinary. He gave her his hand to step down from the carriage and led her himself into the room where the guests were. They all fell silent; the dancing ceased; the violins stopped playing; all eyes rested on the rare beauty of this unknown woman. She had been found.

Because no one knew who she was, the whispers started immediately. "What is her name? Where did she come from?"

Surely the author of the tale didn't call her a rare beauty just because her cheekbones were remarkable. He didn't say that everyone fell silent because the neckline on her gown was jewel studded. Cinderella had a loveliness that radiated from her heart. It shone through her eyes and glowed around her face. She possessed the rare beauty of one who has suffered but remained kind. One who has faced rejection but has not been hardened by it. In the written story, there is no physical description of Cinderella to distract us from the beauty of her heart. The color of her hair and eyes was irrelevant. Why? Because the little girl who sat in the cinders had been discovered by the prince.

She took his hand and they began to dance. His love wrapped around her as warmly and firmly as his arm. She gained assurance and poise from his confident steps. She followed his lead and responded to his attention. The violins came in again, and the couple waltzed as if they had known each other all their lives . . .

Ahem, back to real life . . . Cut the music. Would the dancers please clear the floor? The story is over. Let's come back to earth now . . . We all have laundry to do.

It's hard to let our hearts explore too deeply into the story of Cinderella before something inside cuts us off—namely, the dungeon and our doubts. We hit our heads on the ceiling of this fairy-tale world because, once again, it doesn't match our world. Sure love might begin like that, we tell ourselves, but it won't last. Our cynicism comes up from the dungeon and refuses to let us cooperate with the notion of being so deeply loved for two reasons: First, because we've never known a prince like that. Second, because we've never been loved like that.

WE'VE NEVER KNOWN A PRINCE LIKE THAT

Men deserve a book of their own dedicated to keeping the heart of a prince in this not-so-fairy-tale world. They have their own difficulties finding their paths. How does a man continue to value character and virtue and nobility in the midst of a culture that seldom praises him for much beyond his image?

In his book *The Image,* Daniel Boorstin wrote, "It used to be that a man was famous because he was great; now a man is seen as great because he is famous." The contrast of those two is staggering. Before television, the public image of a man didn't contribute anything to his greatness; it was merely a by-product of the greatness that was there. But now a man (or woman) becomes a celebrity by appearing in the newspapers, movies, television, and, our most recent addition, on the Internet. People who have done nothing to achieve real greatness are famous simply because they are recognized. Figures who never would have had fame are now in the media every day. We notice that their lives are empty of real achievement, but they are not known for real achievement. Instead, they are well known for their well-knownness. The celebrity has taken the place of the hero in our modern world.

The media continue to beat the bushes for the next star who will rush to the top of the heap, only to be at the bottom by the next season. But the hero will remain a timeless figure. A hero is defined in sacred texts and history books; a celebrity is defined by public opinion, magazines, and movie screens. Or through television shows that make today's man famous for the number of women vying for his love in a public competition. Boorstin notes, "The hero [or the prince] is a big man, and the celebrity is a big name."

We've also met the antihero—the man celebrated and praised for having no heroic characteristics whatsoever. We've championed his "nothingness" brought out in sitcoms and movies. When tragedy strikes, the antihero makes us laugh by running away, even knocking people down to get out first. The antihero models the road to destruction, showing men what it looks like to lose hope, to give up, or to destroy their lives with addictions they are powerless to overcome. What happens to a prince when he spends his time watching people no one can admire or respect?

A man can hire a press agent to blow hot air into the empty balloon of a big name, but no agent can ever make a man great or give him his real name. Unless a man aspires to truly great things, he will never become a real hero at all.

Her building was on fire. Something had exploded several floors underneath them. They heard the blast and then were knocked to the ground by what must have been several floors collapsing. There may have been an earthquake. She tried to crawl to her desk, but nothing was where it had been just a minute ago. She could see the shattered glass doors of the office suite, and she wondered where Marjorie was. The elderly receptionist had just walked through those doors seconds before, coming from the elevator. Her head was pounding, and smoke was filling the room. She needed to find Marjorie, but she couldn't stand up. There was a spike of pain around her knee, and she realized something had fallen on her leg.

Later she would tell the reporter that she must have passed out. She remembered being on her hands and knees, searching for Marjorie. But she didn't remember finding Marjorie's body and holding her hand. She didn't remember being carried out of the building. And sadly, she couldn't remember the name of the prince who had come for her.

In our world of big names, true princes are too often anonymous. They are men with solid virtues who are admired for far more than their public image, because they don't have a public image. They remain princes precisely because no one knows who they are.

On September 11, 2001, it again became easy to recognize some of them. The veil was lifted, and we could see glimpses of the invisible kingdom. Our minimum-wage, Timex-watched firemen stood shoulder to shoulder with the Rolexed corporate types, demonstrating hearts of heroes and princes. Not empty suits, these had real hearts in them. These men were not celebrities showing up for the camera—the cameras were showing up to capture images of princes in disguise, real heroes with arms and legs who didn't run away in the face of danger. We may laugh at the antihero on a sitcom, but it wouldn't be funny at all to be seated next to one on a flight that was being hijacked.

And it is not only firemen or those who perform "heroic" tasks that are princes. A man may be a banker or a teacher; he may sell insurance, drive a truck, or drive his wife crazy on Saturdays. But if he is a prince in his heart first, then people will know far more about who he is in life than what he does for a living.

"Some day my prince will come" is not merely a fairy-tale lyric for a romantic waltz. Women want to waltz with the heart of a prince every day in practical ways. We desire his saving love in ordinary aspects of life—after a long day with the kids, in a medical crisis, or through his daily provision from meaningful work. A man has opportunities every day to be a prince. Whether it is to his wife, his mother, or his girlfriend, he will demonstrate his princely heart by finding her and loving her, over and over again.

WE'VE NEVER BEEN LOVED LIKE THAT

The second reason we find it hard to identify with Cinderella's prince is because many of us have never been loved like that. We aren't sure whether it is because we aren't beautiful enough, or because we did so many things wrong when we were younger, or maybe because we really just aren't lovable in the first place. Whatever reason we fabricate, we fear we will never have a love that dances with our hearts and speaks peace to our souls. Better to get on to the errands and stop daydreaming.

Why would a woman trust a love that she has never known? It's far easier to leave the happy story of Cinderella to the little girls and get back to business or to dismiss Cinderella as a poor misguided girl who just wanted to be the center of attention than to allow ourselves to imagine that *we* could be the one at the ball. Better to forget the whole affair.

Don't you think Cindy must have had her doubts too?

As she was racing home and the clock was striking midnight, each toll of the bell took something away from her. The pumpkin carriage smashed into pieces. *But wasn't it a magnificent carriage just minutes ago?* The coachmen returned to their ordinary form of mice and scampered into the night. *Were they really coachmen, or did I dream it?* Then, looking down, she noticed she was back in the same rags as before. Plain old Cinderella. Where had the princess gone? *How could I have been so stupid?*

Cinderella must have faced the same battle in her spirit that we do. What would she do the next day? Would she allow deeper doubt to creep in? Would she question whether she was really ever at the ball? *Was it too good to be true? Was it just a dream? Now do I go back to my real life and forget what just happened? What was I thinking? I'm no princess! Look at all this work I have to do . . .* She could land herself in the dungeon in no time.

Or she could have arrogantly marched into her stepsister's room, taken some of the clothes out of her closet, and claimed them for her own. She could have now thought, *After all I am a princess. No, you don't see it now, but you should have seen me last night. Everyone loved me. I was the talk of the ball—the prince noticed me, not you.* She could now demanded that her stepsisters treat her better. She could have announced that princes from all over would soon be beating down the door.

Cinderella may have had deep questions; the story doesn't say. But she had one thing that helped her silence the doubts, enabling her to stay out of the dungeon and away from a castle in the air. Cinderella had a shoe. For whatever reason, everything turned from the extraordinary back to the ordinary and wretched *except the glass slipper*. The slipper was still real. So Cinderella tucked it away and continued as before. She had no idea what would come next, but she knew she was different on the inside. And when she doubted, she could look at the glass slipper and know it hadn't been a dream. She had danced with the prince in that shoe, and she would never be the same.

She only had one shoe. There was nothing to boast in, to show off. The hidden glass slipper was proof that would never convince the world. But Cinderella didn't need to convince the world—she needed only to remind her heart.

Through his practice, Paul Tournier, the Swiss psychologist, saw many women as modern Cinderellas. He saw them as heroes of unmarked devotion, exploited by everyone all their lives. Invisible, with no one paying any attention to them as persons. Trampled upon, they sit alone in the ashes of sadness and doubt the value of their existence. Feeling as though they are only here to perform services for others, they have no idea what they really want in life. Tournier found great joy in playing the part of the fairy godmother by reviving a Cinderella who had been crushed since childhood. By recognizing her, he could begin to speak tenderly to her heart and send her out to meet the Real Prince.

Cinderella never had a name that fit her. She wasn't in a family that fit her. Not until the prince gave her the shoe that fit her: Adoration. Now the name Cinderella conjures up the picture of a beautiful princess. Now we know she is part of a magnificent royal family. The little girl sitting in the ashes wasn't able to see what could become of her life until she met the prince. Love redeemed her name.

MEET THE PRINCE WHO LOVES LIKE THAT

He was at a friend's house when she came in. She was a mess. She'd been crying and couldn't hold it all together. She had to walk by people in the house to find him. She could hear their whispers, "What's she doing here?" The other women were more than curious— "Who is *she* looking for?"—each afraid it might be her husband. But she just kept on until she saw him.

Then she couldn't keep from sobbing. She couldn't speak, but there was no need for words. It was obvious what she was saying. Everyone in the room knew the woman kissing his feet was for sale. Perhaps some of the men had bought before and felt nervous with her there. They wanted him to stop her from carrying on. One man standing near the scene was thinking, *If this man were a prince, he would be able to recognize a princess, and she ain't it.*

But the invisible kingdom reveals a different version.

She walked in the door, and all of heaven fell silent. The dancing ceased. The violins stopped playing. All eyes rested on the rare beauty of this unknown woman. She had been found.

The whispers started immediately. "He sees her."

As she approached him, he alone could see into her heart. He alone knew what God had named her. He alone could feel the pain of where she had been. And despite her tears, he alone could see the beauty she would become. He knew she was a princess because she was a daughter of the King. The prince recognized her, took her by the hand, led her out on the floor, and danced with her in front of everyone. Mouths fell open. The crowd couldn't fathom the kind of love that would cause the Prince of all heaven to dance with a prostitute princess.

This is the kind of love that finds and rescues.

The Prince of heaven is the truest prince who ever lived—the Son of God. Sent to invite us to enter the invisible kingdom. Sent to change our lives forever by his great love. His desire is that not one person should die without knowing his love. He knows what our hearts long for. And he smiles as he sees what happens to our hearts when we are loved.

We don't have to wait any longer to be found. We can stop hoping that someone else will come and rescue us. He has already found us and rescued us, and our hearts are set free to skip and dance and respond to his love. It's what we were made for. Love has redeemed our name.

THE PRINCE WILL NEVER BE *THE PRINCE*

He was on his cell phone in Starbucks. I was at the next table, which put us two inches apart, so I heard more than I wanted to. "Why do we have to go into this right now?" There was silence as she spoke. "Can't we discuss it when I get home?" I wondered if she would give. "I know, but I've got to finish the report by 2:00."

She decided not to wait until he got home, and she launched into arguing and laying out her case. I could tell because he slightly rolled his eyes and waited . . . "Yes, I am upset. I just show it differently." Silence again. "Don't cry . . ."

And then, "Why are you so mad at me?" Long pause. "I'll be home around 2:30 . . . I know I said 2:00, but we've been on the phone for thirty minutes, and I have to finish this report by 2:00. I don't want to talk about it anymore. I'll be there as soon as I can." He hung up the phone and hung his head.

The woman at home will probably never know this, but he cried.

Women put men under enormous pressure to be the prince. Most of the time we aren't even aware of how much we do it. Somewhere along the journey we stopped hoping that the prince would come and started hoping that the prince would come through. The hope of his physical presence changed into a demand for his emotional presence.

Some of those expectations are normal and right. But if a woman doesn't yet know her own name, or if she thinks that the love she has (or doesn't have) is all the love there is, she might end up clutching the prince by the throat. Every woman seeks to get the love she needs from an earthly prince, but at some level it will not satisfy her—ever. The thirst for love in a woman's heart must be met first by a higher love, from a well that won't run dry. Unfortunately, an earthly prince just doesn't have that much water.

And neither does a princess. A princess can't make a man a prince by marrying him, any more than she could put him in the garage and make him a car. Marriage doesn't determine a prince; it reveals him. Sadly, many a princess has married a toad that stayed a toad. And equally sad, just as many princes have married beautiful women they thought were princesses, who never turned into anything but demanding.

So the princess must first look into the face of God's Son. She must trust her love from the Prince of heaven above the love of any earthly prince. Whether she is single, married, divorced with three children, or a young teenager entering the world of love, she must turn her gaze to meet his eyes before looking into the eyes of anyone else.

THE LOOK OF LOVE

The look of Jesus will mean a broken heart forever from allegiance to any other person or thing. Has Jesus ever looked at you? The look of Jesus transforms and transfixes. Where you are "soft" with God is where the Lord has looked at you.
—OSWALD CHAMBERS

A princess heart stays soft and kind when the love of the Prince is allowed access. The places where our hearts are hard and vindictive or insistent on their own way indicate areas that have not yet been transformed by his gaze. When his eyes of love fall on the hard spots in our hearts, the hardness melts away. The Prince looks at the rugged rocks that have formed in our hearts from years of holding grudges and asks, "May I have those? You won't be needing them." His peaceful eyes turn the key on the irons of wrath in our hearts, setting us free to forgive others. His gaze falls on our sins, and for once we are able to confess them openly, rather than defensively excusing them.

TRUSTING THE LOVE OF THE PRINCE

The airline left my bag in Atlanta when I flew to England. I had been wearing the same clothes for three days, hoping each day my suitcase would arrive. Everyone in the manor was beginning to feel sorry for me while giving me a wide berth in the hallway. Dinner in the dining room was a formal affair, and I didn't have anything to wear except my blue jeans, so I ate in my room the first two nights, although the hostess and the waiter went out of their way to invite me into the dining room.

I wanted to walk into the candlelit room with white tablecloths in my three-day-old clothes, but I lacked the internal confidence. I feared others in the restaurant who were dressed appropriately would think I was an American who didn't know better. So I politely declined dinner for the third time and went instead to the little dovecote upstairs where I did most of my writing. I hadn't been there long when the waiter appeared with a white tablecloth and a candle for me. He brought dinner to my small, upstairs corner. I dined like a princess in my three-day-old clothes. I didn't deserve it. I had let the old whispers of Warwick get the best of me, but the Prince came looking for me once again.

Keeping a princess heart is not about living in luxury. We can surround ourselves with beautiful things, deny ourselves no privilege or pleasure, and still never understand what it is to be named by the King and cherished by the Prince. Things cannot comfort us; they don't know how. Things cannot love us; they are not capable. Once we know that the Prince loves our hearts, things can bring comfort to us, but only because we first know we are loved. Love at the core makes all the difference.

Trusting the Prince is never forced. He doesn't make us obey him. He looks at us with the tender eyes that first found us, and we follow him. In the same way, we trust him with our lives. Who else could love us like that? Who else knows us as he does? We could follow others, but why? The princess's response to him is, "Whatever you ask of me I will do."

When we have a problem trusting, we don't need to brush up on the rules of how to trust; we need to get better acquainted with the one we are trying to put our trust in. When a woman sees a doctor about a heart condition, she listens to what the doctor says about how to lower her cholesterol. If she believes him, she trusts him. She will not say, "No butter? You won't let me have any butter? Listening to you is just about following rules." What the doctor says means something to her, and what the doctor is telling her to do is what is best for her heart. She trusts that the doctor's intentions are good toward her and that his goal is to take care of her.

God loves us more than any doctor. We can take him at his word. We don't look to a flower to determine whether "he loves me, he loves me not." There is no running debate. We can hold our heads high as daughters of the King, loved by the greatest Prince of all time. Neither honor has come to us as a result of our doing. Each is bestowed on us as a free gift from the invisible kingdom.

The princess heart can rest in her belovedness. And when she doubts, she looks at the glass slipper on her dresser. She has it. It's still there. Yes, he loves her. She doesn't have to prove it or show it off or wear it. She need only trust in her name and in his love and keep walking. And when someone asks, "Hey, Cinderella, does the shoe fit you now?" She can answer with confidence, "Yes, by grace, it does indeed."

A princess heart can rest in the truth that her Prince has come. He loves her and cherishes her. And she believes that one day, in the twinkling of an eye, the Prince is coming again. And when he comes again, it's for forever. And it's not for a dance this time—it's for a wedding.

CHAPTER EIGHT

Happily Ever After

She tumbled into bed about midnight and finally fell asleep, wishing the world were a better place, wishing there was more good news to report, and most of all, wishing the kids hadn't watched an earlier newscast with her, which had included a terrorist bombing, a murder, and the kidnapping of a little boy.

Now it's 3:30 in the morning, and her four-year-old is patting her on her arm. She sits up in bed, trying to focus on his face in the dark. He is sniffling softly. "What is it, honey?" The little boy remains silent. She reaches for her bathrobe at the foot of the bed, picks him up, and heads down the hall toward his room. As she lays him back in his bed, his crying intensifies. She asks again, "What is it?" His little lip quivers, and he looks toward the wall, not wanting to say. "Are you scared?" she suggests. He nods and cries harder. "Can you tell me? Do you know what you're afraid of?" He shrugs his shoulders.

She takes her little son into her arms and kisses the top

157

of his head. "It's okay," she whispers into his hair. "Whatever it is, it's going to be okay." She holds him, lost in her own thoughts. Is it really going to be okay? Can I promise him that? Should I tell him Mommy wonders the same thing sometimes?

She has calmed his fears so easily, so confidently—so instinctively. In her heart she deeply believes "all will be well," but in her head she isn't quite sure how she can promise it. She looks lovingly at her son, who has finally fallen asleep, snuggled in the warmth of her reassurances. And she pads back to her own room, praying for some reassurances of her own.

All too often our life experiences do not successfully add up to "happily ever after." People we love have died, circumstances have devastated us, evil has won stunning short-term victories over good, and we have been left with doubts about love's ability to conquer all. Yet even after being buried under questions or submerged in fear and cynicism, the most timeless desire of our hearts has a way of bobbing to the surface, glimmering with hope.

At the very center of human life is a deep trust in the order of things. If we didn't have this trust, we would not view the ultimate outcome of our personal stories as loving or joyful or peaceful but as terrifying. Without some innate sense of order, we would never be able to reassure our children, "It's going to be okay." Unless we maintain a firm belief in the ultimate triumph of good over evil, we have no assurance of anything.

Was the mother in the previous story lying to her son when she told him he didn't need to be afraid? Or did she somehow trust, even in her own tired and troubled state, that whatever had happened, whatever was wrong, it would be made right? We instinctively offer comfort to our children. Even mothers with no faith in God provide promises and reassurances. They may not be entirely sure on what grounds they can give them, but they do it anyway. Because deep inside their hearts, they hold the same hope as people of faith: that death does not have the final word, that evil will not ultimately win, and that love will conquer all.

This is the deepest longing of our hearts: the desire that *all will be well.*

THE BEAUTY OF SLEEPING BEAUTY

The story starts happily and innocently with the birth of Princess Aurora. But when the evil sister of the king is not invited to the baby girl's christening, the trouble begins. The day of celebration comes, and the friends and family speak blessings over the little princess. Then the jealous aunt arrives. She blows in like a dark cloud and pronounces a curse before anyone has a chance to stop her. She decrees that the princess will prick her finger on a spinning wheel and die before her sixteenth birthday. Needless to say, the celebration turns dark, and happiness turns to mourning.

One of the other aunts steps in. While she cannot undo the curse, she can cancel the power of death. She declares that when the girl pricks her finger, instead of dying she will fall asleep. It will be a sleep like death and will last for a hundred years. But at the end of that time a king's son will come and wake her, and she will live. In the meantime, all the others vow to do their best to protect the princess and make sure she never pricks her finger. They decide to tuck her away for safety and to rid the kingdom of all spinning wheels. Everyone feels a little better, and the party resumes.

Life goes on in the castle for years, and the curse is all but forgotten. The princess continues to grow and become more beautiful and kind. Then, on her sixteenth birthday, just as predicted, the princess pricks her finger and falls asleep.

There is terrible sadness in the kingdom. A few remember the old curse and are able to explain to the others what has happened, but that provides little comfort. Even if the curse is only for a hundred years, she is gone. For who will live long enough to see her again? Meanwhile, how many people do you think told the king that his daughter would never wake up? Or implied that he was in denial because he believed that she would?

Time passed, and around the castle it grew harder for anyone to remember the princess at all. Some parents passed on the story to their children, but few believed the promise that the spell would be broken after a hundred years. The ones who did believe had no proof, and others gossiped that they were crazy. Once the king died, no one kept count of the years at all, and the world just kept on going. Those few who still remembered knew that whatever might happen wasn't going to happen in their lifetime, so they might as well give up. It looked as though all was lost.

THE IMPORTANCE OF THE ENDING

I write stories in my head a lot. Watching people in an airport, at a restaurant, in a department store, and even at the gym always prompts me to create a little story line about why someone is there or what people are facing in their lives. You can pick up subtle hints just by watching. At times I've made myself laugh out loud over some silly scenario, or I've been on the edge of tears as I envisioned the possible tragedy occurring in someone's life.

When a couple is saying good-bye at the airport, I might think about their next meeting and then write the ending of their love story in my head. I notice the way he looks around at others, while her gaze stays fixed on him, and I'm certain he will break up with her soon. When I see a mother traveling with her children, I often wonder if she's heading to a place that will give her a break. Later when we all get off the plane and her mother is waiting at the gate, I decide in my story whether grandma has been at home eagerly getting ready for her daughter's arrival or, instead, dreading the intrusion of three little ones into her "space." I watch the businessman conducting a meeting in-between flights, and I wonder if he really believes in what he's selling or if he's just trying to make a living. The clues to the story are there if you look for them.

I don't think I'm alone in this. We all write silent scripts in our heads. When something funny happens at the dry cleaners, we think of how we might later recount it in detail to a friend. When our kids tell us about an event at school, in our minds we race ahead of them, trying to figure out how it's going to end. The clues to the ending are always in the story.

Robert McKee, in his screenwriting book *Story,* underscores the importance of a good ending, one full of meaning. He asserts that if he could send a telegram to all the film producers of the world, it would say, "'Meaning Produces Emotion,' not money; not sex; not special effects; not movie stars; not lush photography." I agree. If you want to capture our hearts with a real story, don't show us the money on the screen; show us the meaning in the script.

When we write in our journals or in our thoughts or even in books, it is all an effort to recognize meaning in the events of life. We review our day in our journals, or we rewind our husband's account of his clash with the boss, or we write a short essay or poem or story—

all to figure out or sort out or wring out the signifi-
cance hidden in the events of our days. We're trying to
answer the question: *What does all this mean?* And
sometimes we write to confess that we just don't see
the meaning at all.

When we can't see the present meaning, then the
future ending takes on a greater importance. *How will
all this turn out? If I can't see the reasons in the short term,
show me what I'm missing by giving me the long view. I
can understand the meaning if I can see the ending.*
Women don't say, "Show me the money." We say,
"Show me the ending. Don't leave me hanging. Show
me where this is going, and then I'll agree to go. Just
don't ask me to trust in the dark." We women will go
almost anywhere and bear almost any burden if we
understand why we are doing it. You want us to wait—
we'll wait, but first tell us what we are waiting for and
what it means. We can bear almost any "how" if we
believe in the "why."

The ending of a story produces a dramatic change
in values—from the positive to the negative or from
the negative to the positive—but the *meaning* of that
change is what touches an audience. The action that
communicates the change might be a warrior's bloody
battle, fought until no one is left standing, or a simple
task like opening the refrigerator and beginning to
make dinner, but the meaning behind that action is
what makes or breaks the ending.

A good ending must stay true to the story. It cannot

be tacked on. It must be the kind of ending Aristotle praised, one that is both "inevitable and unexpected." It should be inevitable because it must remain true to the story and the world in which its characters live. But at the same time it must be unexpected and imaginative. This is the kind of ending that thrills and delights us, and offers great satisfaction.

Americans take a lot of criticism for liking only happy endings. I don't think this is completely warranted. Happy endings don't always provide the greatest emotional satisfaction, which is what we're after. Real satisfaction comes from an ending that fulfills what the writer has promised all along. From the beginning of the story, the writer whispers to his audience, "This is what you can expect." A good writer interweaves clues throughout the tale. He creates expectation, and to the degree he fulfills it with the ending we are satisfied.

Anyone can write a fake happy ending by giving each character what he or she wants. Likewise, any author can finish a story unhappily by killing everyone off. But the true artist, McKee says, is one who "gives us the emotion he's promised . . . but with a rush of unexpected insight" that he has withheld until this turn at the end. The insight that pours forth delivers the longed-for emotion in a way we never could have foreseen.

Tolkien describes how fairy tales do this so well, often bringing us to a "sudden joyous 'turn'" that in the face of horrific events "denies . . . universal final defeat." This is why we love them. They give us "a fleeting glimpse of Joy, Joy beyond the walls of the world, poignant as grief." Tolkien believed that fairy tales' power lies in the fact that they resonate the true story of Christ's passion and resurrection—the greatest, most complete, most inconceivable, and joyous turn ever.

In the story of our world, the perfect sky is still torn. *Once upon a time . . .* seems long ago and far away. Today's world faces wars, diseases, hunger, and poverty. We see power struggles between political parties and watch institutions created to end abuse harbor the abusers themselves. And when we can't see the meaning, the ending takes on a greater importance.

Amid all the darkness, we can still be people who wait with hope. We can hold on tightly to our longing that good will triumph over evil in the most glorious ending imaginable. We have good reason: The Author of history has been whispering it to us since the beginning of the story. And throughout the centuries, the Author has continued to sprinkle clues of what we can expect. In essence he is saying, "Wait, don't give up. Look at what's ahead." God has shown us that the world should have been otherwise and promised that one day it will be. Jesus was a clear picture of this promise. He revealed heaven to earth as if he were fast-forwarding the story in front of our eyes: erasing sickness, restoring sight, repairing limbs, and even rejecting death. He was foreshadowing a part of the greatest ending of all time.

BACK TO THE BEAUTY . . .

After one hundred years, a prince is traveling back to his father's kingdom. He notices a castle in the distance, covered by a thorn hedge on all sides. He inquires about it, and all people can tell him is that it has been that way for longer than anybody can remember. On his way out of town, he stops a very old peasant man and asks him about the castle. The peasant recounts as much of the story as he can remember. "Uh, something about a curse, a hundred years, and a prince . . ."

That is all he needs to hear. He knows that it is time. Sword in hand, the prince cuts away the thorns and takes the steps two at a time up to the huge door. He enters the castle and climbs the stairs, not entirely sure what he will find. The room is just as it was a hundred years before. And there she is, the one he has come to find. She is sleeping peacefully, as beautiful as she was before the curse stopped her life in its tracks. He stands there for a moment, taking it all in. The world has no idea what is about to happen. He approaches the side of her bed and kneels. He places a gentle kiss on her lips, and her eyes flutter open as she wakes . . .

WE CAN'T SEE IT ALL FROM HERE

When I was visiting England, I found a lot of places deceiving. I could never tell the size of a house or a garden by looking at it from the outside. What appeared to be a mousehole would open up to lots of little rooms and then side rooms and then cupboards. A garden would have an archway that became a path that became a maze that opened up to a table set for tea. I couldn't see everything at one glance. I had to explore it and let it open up in front of me.

This is more than a little foreign to those of us from America. We are not used to such a limited vantage point, nor are we entirely comfortable with it. We like great rooms. Often we walk into a house or a church where the key feature is one huge, cavernous, multi-storied room. The eye can take in most of the details in about thirty seconds. Nothing is hidden or tucked away or out of sight. There is no need to explore anything—it's all right there in front of us.

We've grown used to seeing everything at once. We want to walk into life as if it's a great room and be able to see it all in an instant. But real life is never that way. It is far more like an English cottage, unfolding and revealing itself over time. Because we can't see it all from here, we have to wait for the ending.

WE CAN'T SEE IT ALL NOW

Humanity is stranded in time. We have organized our days into hours and minutes so that we can see change as it occurs. Apart from the need to mark change, there would be no need for time. But God does not operate in our time because he never changes. He does not set his watch by Greenwich, nor is he bound in any way by its constraints. Likewise, he does not view history the way we do, in terms of past, present, and future. Every moment is always the present for him. We view the events of our lives in chronological order because of our understanding of time, but these events are not put in that same order by God. He has the ending in mind at the beginning and the beginning in sight while the ending is unfolding.

It's confusing, I know. C. S. Lewis explained it this way:

> Suppose I am writing a novel. I write, "Mary laid down her work; next moment came a knock at the door!" For Mary who has to live the imaginary time of my story there is no interval between putting down the work and hearing the knock. But I, who am Mary's maker, do not live in that imaginary time at all. Between writing the first half of that sentence and the second, I might sit down for three hours and think steadily about Mary. I could think about Mary as if she were the only character in the book and for as long as I pleased, and the hours I spent in doing so would not appear in Mary's time (the time inside the story) at all.

Most of these concepts are beyond my limited ability to understand, much less explain, but the point remains—God is the Author of the story, and the

Author does not live and operate in our time. Anyone who presumes to know the end of the story or how the Author will bring it to completion will be surprised. We simply can't see it all now. We can't hold the past, present, and future together in our minds, much less in our hands. The ending will be inevitable and unexpected.

BUT WE CAN SEE SOMETHING

Just because we can't see it all at once, and we can't see it all now, doesn't mean that we can't see anything at all or that we should give up. Our limitations shouldn't make us give in to this kind of postmodern thinking: "You can't see it all, so you might as well stop looking. You can't understand the concept of time, so quit waiting for anything. You don't understand the meaning, so that proves there is none." This is why there are no postmodern fairy tales. They would never satisfy us.

That's what Charles Perrault discovered in his retelling of *Little Red Riding Hood*, which was extremely unpopular. In his first release of the story the young girl goes to visit her sick grandmother, bringing cakes and jam. She meets a wolf along the way and makes the unfortunate mistake of telling him where she's headed. The wolf runs on ahead while the little girl picks flowers along the way. The grandmother is not home, and the wolf promptly eats the little girl! End of story. No woodcutter, no grandmother. Pretty brutal. It will probably be a movie next year.

Or how about writing a story of a little princess called Snow Beige? It could be about a girl who is just average at everything. She can never do anything right or wrong, because there is no right or wrong. She steals money from her father, but he understands, so he doesn't press charges. She opens her own bank with the stolen money and buys artwork from Sotheby's. She lives "averagely ever after" in Texas until she sells her autobiography.

Many postmodern philosophies are like high-fashion clothing, sort of luxury thinking for your mind. You can show them off at parties, but they are very difficult to wear in everyday life. And people aren't forced to live out their philosophies, so they don't realize the inconsistencies between what they say they believe in a social setting and what they actually believe when it comes to living it out.

For example, I was sitting in an outdoor café when a college student walked by wearing a shirt pro-claiming "The World Sucks." I would have enjoyed having a spirited conversation with him about why he had drawn such a negative conclusion. I probably would have agreed with him on many points, excluding the conclusion, but here is the discrepancy: He was eating ice cream. And not just any ice cream. It looked like chocolate chip cookie dough ice cream in a waffle cone—with sprinkles! You can't eat sprinkles on something when you believe the world sucks. You just can't. You can think the world sucks, and you can put sprinkles on your waffle cone, but you can't aggressively live out your tee-shirt philosophy and engage in that kind of joyful, delicious behavior. Anyone who proudly proclaims that the world sucks should be denied sprinkles and waffle cones and instead be forced to eat beets all the time.

ALL WILL BE WELL

How can women believe in a happily ever after when there hasn't been a happily ever before? If our hearts live only in the visible kingdom, we will miss the hope of happily ever after, because there seems to be no such thing in the visible kingdom. Because you can trust only what you see in front of you. Apart from faith, which holds forgiveness and thus hope, we've seen how we try to create a happy ending superficially (the castle in the air) or decisively dismiss any happy ending as artificial (the dungeon).

Once again, the invisible kingdom offers us a bifocal perspective. In between a false, pious ending and a hopeless, defeated ending, the invisible kingdom reveals a battle taking place between good and evil. Tolkien describes this state in-between: "No man can estimate what is really happening at the present. . . . All we do know, and that to a large extent by direct experience, is that evil labors with vast power and perpetual success—in vain: preparing always only the soil for unexpected good to sprout in."

For Tolkien and others in the invisible kingdom, no

evil event, however horrible, was ever outside the story of salvation—history. God was and is constantly in the process of bending all events to his purposes. Such understanding doesn't make evil any less evil. As Tolkien put it in *The Silmarillion*, "Evil may yet be good to have been . . . and yet remain evil."

Hundreds of years earlier, in the fourteenth century, God revealed this same truth to Julian of Norwich. A mystic and the first writer in English to be identified as a woman, the King entrusted this princess heart with a very powerful truth:

> All shall be well
> And all shall be well
> And all manner of things shall be well.

Julian was the first to admit that she did not know how it would happen. She even confessed that she found it hard to believe, but she never once backed down from what the King had told her. And for centuries to follow, others have put their trust in the same promise. In the midst of the unexplainable, in the injustice of all that is unfair, in the sadness of everything that is left incomplete, there is peace in this hopeful, unassuming assurance. In the middle of the night, when despair tries to close in, when the diagnosis comes, when the husband leaves, when trouble arrives, or the money goes . . .

All shall be well.

No woman living today knows *when* it will be well or *how* it will be well, but every daughter of the King can believe that it *will* be well. Just as he has named us his daughters, just as he sent us the Prince of Peace, just as he has kept every vow he's made in the past, he has also declared to the heavens . . .

And all shall be well.

We want so badly to tell the Author how we think he should finish the story to our satisfaction. We want to place our orders at the divine diner so we are assured of getting our suffering on the side. But we can't. What we can do is trust the King to do as he promised. Just as we have trusted him with our names and trusted him with our hearts, we can commit ourselves to trust him with the ending.

And all manner of things shall be well.

STAND WITH CONVICTION

Believing in a happy ending is not the same as being an optimist. If our belief is not grounded in truth, it will never sustain us. Enthusiasm will never stand the strain of suffering; only the deeper belief and commitment that we are here for God and his purposes can do this. Because we can't always see what those purposes are.

Anne Lamott said in an *L.A. Times* interview that she has always loved books where people tell the truth. "When people tell the truth, it's like finding an English language station in Morocco."

What a great picture. Here we are in the world, full of its constant noise and crazy commotion. We are in a maze of beliefs, and truth is presented as being merely one's own personal point of view. Everything is shifting and relative. We read the paper or turn on the news, and the pictures and headlines seem either black and tragic or superficial and meaningless. The words and pictures overwhelm us until everything seems like gibberish. We feel lost. Hot and thirsty, we are unable to find our way back to where we were or to locate the road that will get us where we are trying to go.

Eventually we stumble upon the truth. All at once we are handed a cup of water, we can talk to someone who understands, and we can look at a map in our language. All of a sudden we know where we are. We figure out that we're not really lost—we just have to summon our courage, take the next left, and go up two blocks. The truth is a marker in the midst of the chaos—*all will be well.*

STAND WITH COURAGE

To be courageous doesn't mean that you are not afraid; it means that fear doesn't win by changing your course. Courage is staying the course in the face of danger. It is sticking with your intended plan of action in the midst of difficulty or uncertainty, without being overcome by fear. It is holding tight to your convictions when you have doubts. Even when we know *what* to do in the middle of dark uncertainty, we still need courage to *do* it.

A princess translation of 2 Corinthians 4:16–18 might read this way:

> Don't give up! I know it looks as though every-thing is falling apart on the outside. Look with the eyes of your heart at what is happening on the inside. The King is making a new way for you, grace upon grace. What you're going through right now seems crushing, but don't lose sight of what is coming. There is far more ahead than what meets the eye. What you see now will not even be here tomorrow, but what you can't see just yet will last forever.

If we are going to live with a princess heart in a not-so-fairy-tale world, we have to remember that all noble things are difficult. Living in the invisible kingdom is a heroic and holy thing. But the difficulty of it does not make us give up; it inspires us to overcome because our suffering is not wasted. It counts for something. What we are going through is strengthening us in a way that helps us. The King will continue to supply us with the courage and the grace not only to survive, but to grow stronger.

Like Sleeping Beauty we are living under a curse that we cannot change. But unlike the dreamy princess, we are not asleep. We are wide-awake and can fully participate in our own story. We are not still waiting for our prince; we are in a daily relationship with him. And although the rich and meaningful life we are looking for is possible, it will not just happen. A string of days in succession on the calendar with too much to do will happen to us—but a life of meaning is something we have to pursue. Whatever ingredients are still in the fridge on a Friday night is what happens to us—but the meal we make from those ingredients is something we have to create. The things that shaped our hearts in the past have happened to us, but the kind of heart that comes from those things—a princess heart—is something we have to choose.

ONCE UPON A DREAM

I met Sleeping Beauty on an airplane. I was sitting in my seat, minding my own business, writing about princesses, when I heard the flight attendant exclaim, "Sleeping Beauty? Really?" I turned around and peered over the top of my seat to see Mary Costa. I never would have recognized her name, but she was the voice of Sleeping Beauty in the 1959 Walt Disney film. I was born in the sixties, and this was the version I grew up with. The woman sitting behind me was the voice of the fairy-tale princess I knew and loved. And looking at her over the seat, I could tell that Disney must have modeled the face of the princess after her beauty.

I could hardly believe it. I introduced myself and

told her I was working on a book about keeping a princess heart in a not-so-fairy-tale world. I hadn't thought how she might react to such a concept and title. She clapped her hands in delight and said it sounded wonderful. And without really thinking again, I handed her a rough draft of a chapter. Inside I probably just wanted to back up what must have sounded like a made-up story to her. I thought she might take a polite look and hand it back, but every time I turned around, she was still reading. I kept thinking, *She's a princess, a real live princess, and she's reading my chapter!* She read the whole thing. I asked Mary if I might send her a copy of the book when I was finished, and she said, "Yes, I have to see how it turns out." It was hard to sit still on the rest of the flight with Sleeping Beauty wide awake behind me.

A few weeks later I got a large envelope in the mail. Mary had sent me a picture of Sleeping Beauty, with this inscription:

> *To beautiful princess Nicole—*
> *A rare gift to this world.*
> *With love and deepest admiration,*
> —MARY COSTA

I felt as if I had won the lottery. Actually I felt a lot like Callie Randall, the princess in her pajamas. Along with the picture, Mary had sent me a note, saying, "If we are daughters of the king, then we are sisters. I like that."

I do too, Mary Costa. I do too.

Not only does she have a princess voice, she clearly has a princess heart.

I have no idea how her life has turned out. I don't know whether she married a prince or if she's had to face breast cancer. I don't know if she's lost a child or has a castle full of them, but I could tell in our brief encounter that whatever her circumstances have been, she isn't the least bit burned out or bitter in her spirit. She's kept a princess heart. It seemed so obvious to me that after all these years, and whatever life has offered her, she still believes in happily ever after.

So do I, Mary Costa. So do I.

PRINCESS HEARTS AND HAPPILY EVER AFTER

As we mature, we will face more and more of life, and we will also taste more and more of death. We will bury more loved ones, lose more dreams, and weather more storms. We will feel the inevitable incompleteness that life on earth offers. But in the invisible kingdom, every death brings new life. The death of our little dreams calls us to find bigger ones: the kind of dreams that can't be stained or tainted or stolen by the world. As we lose, or turn loose of some of those lesser dreams, we find we can replace them with dreams that are truly alive and are somehow older, as we are. We may think them less satisfying in the short run, but what they are lifting us toward will satisfy us forever.

In my mind's eye I can see a salt-and-pepper-haired stockbroker going into a meeting with a new awareness that she is a princess. None of her colleagues will notice a difference at first, but it won't take long. She stands a little taller and smiles much brighter, knowing that she is worth far more than the number of shares she sells. She gives her best in the presentation she makes, understanding for the first time in her life that the presentation doesn't make her. Her young, working-class dream was to grow wealthy and be surrounded with things of great value. Now her heart has found its own wealth and is dreaming of how to be of great value to the world. Now she has a name, Princess, and that means everything.

I can see another princess standing with a cane by the window. The bones in her hand are delicate and pronounced but still strong. She is looking at the sunset, the way she used to look for her son. He doesn't come to visit the facility as often as he used to. A few years ago she dreamed that he would step in and fill the empty places left by her husband's death. She is alone now but rarely feels the throbbing of loneliness. Every day she meets with the Prince of heaven, and her royal heart is growing stronger in his love. She stands expectantly in the glow of the setting sun, but she's not waiting for a human visitor. Her princess heart smiles an eighty-year-old smile and thinks, *Someday soon my Prince will come.*

I can see a beautiful young mother making peanut-butter-and-jelly sandwiches. Years before, in college, she had been found and loved by a prince. Not so long ago she lost the prince in a plane crash. All of her young-girl dreams of Saturdays together and Christmas mornings as a family went down with him. But her princess heart had already learned to dream bigger dreams and to trust the King with every aspect of her future. So as she puts the top slice of bread on the sandwiches and cuts away the crusts the way they like it, she wipes away tears of deep sadness, but her princess heart holds tighter than ever to the ultimate happily ever after.

A vision from the apostle John of the day of our dreams . . .

I saw a new heaven and a new earth, for the first heaven and the first earth had passed away. Also there was no more sea. Then I, John, saw the holy city, New Jerusalem, coming down out of heaven from God, prepared as a bride adorned for her husband. And I heard a loud voice from heaven saying, "Behold the tabernacle of God is with men, and He will dwell with them, and they shall be His people. . . . And God will wipe away every tear from their eyes; there shall be no more death, nor sorrow, nor crying; and there shall be no more pain, for the former things have passed away." Then He who sat on the throne said, "Behold, I make all things new." And He said to me, "Write, for these words are true and faithful." And He said to me, "It is done! I am the Alpha and the Omega, the Beginning and the End." (Revelation 21:1–6 NKJV)

His words are true and faithful. He will make all things new. The Author of history will proclaim, "It is done. The Beginning has met the End." The inevitable will meet the unexpected, and our joy will be boundless. We will understand what all of his promises meant. As we look back to the beginning from the end, we will see the meaning of the story.

The princesses will join the King. I can see us gathering around, his ragtag band of daughters, called out and named by him, loved by the Prince, and secure in the ending. A single glass slipper here, a tarnished tiara there, a strand of pearls with just a few still intact. Stories to tell, griefs to share, joys to celebrate. Some of us are walking, others limping, and some leaping. Though we are scarred and maimed from our trials and battles, though we are weary and wounded, we are more beautiful than ever, anticipating living out the grandest happily ever after of all time.

With gratitude to the amazing princesses and princes in disguise who dress down every day as ordinary people and surround me with friendship, love, and support.

Lela Gilbert, my trusted editor, who helped excavate this book from the marble block of my thoughts and helped bring the princess into beautiful sight.

Debbie Wickwire, Allen Arnold and my entire publishing team at Thomas Nelson whose consistent encouragement and support took an idea and made it look like this.

Mary Graham, whose incredible leadership of Women of Faith is fueled by her princess heart and warms my heart in friendship every day. How I love you.

Luci Swindoll, whose princess heart is the greatest adventure I've known.

Luci, Sheila, Marilyn, Thelma, and Patsy, my sisters

and friends on the team who are helping thousands of women every year find their name—thank you for helping me find mine. Words are not enough, but they are a good start. You all mean the world to me.

A special word to Angela Thomas, a wonderful author, mother, and trusted friend. In the invisible kingdom, we live side by side. Your friendship reigns in my heart. And to Audrey Adams, your friendship provides coffee and communion full of the deepest and richest blends.

My creative team of Mary Bowman, Amy Cella, Mashea Richards, and David and Leah Simmons. I would be lost without your continued support and hard work. Your tireless dedication and commitment to the Lord are not invisible to me. I see, and I'm so very grateful. I love working with each of you.

The design team of David Riley and his fabulous associates for their creative work on the cover. Thanks for making the outside reflect the inside so well.

My family, spread out from Alabama to Australia and many places in-between. Your kindness, love and prayers have sustained me through many difficult days. See you soon.

While many princes are brothers, not all brothers are princes. A special thank you to my brothers, Bruce and John, for loving me so well.

For my parents with love and gratitude for giving me the very best gifts life has to offer: faith, hope, and love. But the greatest of these is love.

An Anthology. 1978. George MacDonald. ed. C. S. Lewis. New York: MacMillan.

Chronicles of Narnia. 1955. C. S. Lewis. New York: MacMillan.

George MacDonald and His Wife Greville M. MacDonald with an Introduction by GK Chesterton. 1924. George MacDonald. London: G. Allen & Unwin.

Heaven is Not My Home. 1998. Paul Marshall. Nashville: Word Publishing.

My Utmost for His Highest. 1997. Oswald Chambers. Chicago: Moody Press.

Of Other Worlds: Essays and Stories. 1967. C. S. Lewis. ed. Walter Hooper. New York Harcourt. Brace & World.

Something Beautiful for God. 1986. Malcolm Muggeridge. San Francisco: Harper.

Story. 1997. Robert McKee. New York: HarperCollins.

The Business of Heaven. Daily Readings. 1984. C. S. Lewis. San Diego: Harcourt Brace Jovanovich.

The Complete Fairy Tales of Charles Perrault. 1993. New York: Clarion.

The Four Loves. 1991. C. S. Lewis. New York: Harcourt Brace.

The Image. 1961. Daniel Boorstin. New York: Random House.

The Lost Princess. 1990. George MacDonald. Oregon: Harvest House.

The Magnificent Obsession. 1932. Lloyd Douglas. New York: Willett. Clark. & Company.

The Spirit of the Disciplines. 1991. Dallas Willard. San Francisco: Harper.

The Southern Belle Primer. 1991. Maryln Schwartz. New York: Doubleday.

The Princess and the Goblin. 1999. George MacDonald. New York: Dover Publications.

The Princess and Curdie. 1934. George MacDonald. Philadelphia: D. McKay.

The Tolkien Reader. 1966. J. R. R. Tolkien. New York: Ballatine Books.

The Weight of Glory. 2000. C. S. Lewis. San Francisco: Harper SanFrancisco.

What's in a Name? 1975. Paul Tournier. London: SCM Press.

*W*hen **Nicole Johnson** takes the stage, audiences don't know if they're about to laugh or cry—but they know something special is about to happen. Dramatist and author of six books (including *Keeping a Princess Heart in a Not-So-Fairy-Tale World*, *Fresh Brewed Life*, and *The Invisible Woman*), Nicole's one-woman dramatic presentations combine comedy with God's wisdom, giving rich insights into daily life. Nicole has also demonstrated her abilities as a host on the Hallmark Channel on the show *Midpoint* and in a Time Life infomercial called *The Folk Years*. She lives in California with her husband.

Nicole Johnson's
Five-Year DVD Collection

Nicole's complete collection of DVDs spans five years of her live performances. This set includes all the sketches from *No Place Like Hope*, *Keeping a Princess Heart*, *Stepping Into the Ring*, *Funny Stuff Women Can Relate To*, and *Just a Touch of Faith*.

> **SKETCHES INCLUDE:**
> Princess in Pajamas • Faith on Channel 5 • A Touch of Faith • First and Goal • T2: Tammi Jean Returns • The Waiting Room • Stretch Out Your Hand • Keeping a Princess Heart • Girlfriends • The Invisible Woman • Raising the Sail • Hats • When I Was Little • Rocks • Don't Tell Anyone • Boundless Love • Motherhood • What Am I Going to Wear? • The Proverbs 31 Woman • Stepping Into the Ring

www.freshbrewedlife.com

The Faith, Hope, and Love Trilogy

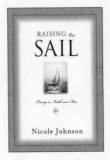

RAISING THE SAIL

Just as sailboats are made for the wind, women are made for relationships—and with both it takes faith to overcome the fear to let go and trust God's direction. Instead of frantically paddling or "motoring" our way through the seas of our emotional connections with each other, Nicole challenges us to freely let go and trust the "Windmaker," God Himself, to help us find our way.

STEPPING INTO THE RING

Where is the woman old or young who will not shed a tear and silently scream in her heart as she walks in these pages through the diagnosis of breast cancer and the devastation that ensues? While she focuses on the specific soul-chilling crisis, Nicole offers her readers broader insights for dealing with major losses of all kinds. She extends genuine hope and much-needed rays of light to those who are mired in hopelessness and despair.

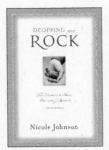

DROPPING YOUR ROCK

You can express your moral outrage by joining the angry mob howling for a sinner to be stoned. But what if that sinner is your friend and you would rather change their heart than shed their blood? We don't have to hurl the rocks we clutch in our judgmental hands. With tender words and touching photos, Nicole Johnson guides us toward the "flat thud of grace" that can change our lives when we drop our rocks and choose to love instead.

Dramatic Encounters with God

Walk with Christ through ancient Jerusalem as he encounters the man with the withered hand, John the Baptist, Judas, and four other New Testament characters in this book of dramatic sketches by Nicole Johnson, the Women of Faith® dramatist. Nicole uses her talent for storytelling to help us be there with Christ and see the scenes with new eyes and understanding, bringing to life lessons that apply to our modern lives.

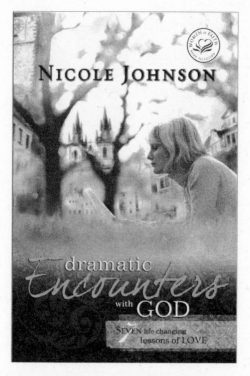

Hardcover ISBN 10: 0-8499-0357-2,
ISBN 13: 978-0-8499-0357-1

*W*ith wit and wisdom, Nicole Johnson leads the reader in a journey of awakenings—first, to God as you respond to His tender, passionate love for you; second to yourself as you embrace your identity as a woman, your gifts, and your dreams; finally, to others as you learn to love and communicate in ways that bring joy and closeness.

Nicole offers a freshly-brewed, heartwarming wake-up-and-smell-the-coffee guide to living life to the fullest. She encourages Christian women to recognize the areas in their lives where they are sound asleep—and let God wake them up again.

Challenging and immensely practical, *Fresh-Brewed Life* is a heartwarming book that's good to the last drop—good enough to change your life and help you touch the lives of others.

Hardcover ISBN 10: 0-7852-6951-7, ISBN 13: 978-0-7852-6951-9
Trade Paper ISBN 10: 0-7852-6704-2, ISBN 13: 978-0-7852-6704-1

WOMEN OF FAITH®

Women of Faith, North America's largest women's conference, is an experience like no other. Thousands of women — all ages, sizes, and backgrounds — come together in arenas for a weekend of love and laughter, stories and encouragement, drama, music, and more. The message is simple. The result is life-changing.

What this conference did for me was to show me how to celebrate being a woman, mother, daughter, grandmother, sister or friend.
— Anne, Corona, CA

I appreciate how genuine each speaker was and that they were open and honest about stories in their life—even the difficult ones.
— Amy, Fort Worth, TX

GO, you MUST go. The Women of Faith team is wonderful, uplifting, funny, blessed. Don t miss out on a chance to have your life changed by this incredible experience.
— Susan, Hartford, CT